WHO'S ENGAGED?
CLIMB THE LEARNING LADDER TO SEE

JANET K. PILCHER

Book Cover Design and Graphics by Matt Behnke at SeeLevel Graphics, Pensacola, Florida

Acknowledgements

- Dr. Robin Largue, the co-author of *How to Lead Teachers to Become Great*, provided tremendous help and guidance to me each step of the way as I wrote *Who's Engaged*. She helped this book move from an idea to a reality. Robin and I work with teachers and leaders to apply the *Student Engagement Framework* and good leadership skills that improve performance. My partnership with her has great value in what I do each day.
- I deeply appreciate Mr. Quint Studer for giving me an opportunity to feel that I have purpose, do worthwhile work, and make a difference in the lives of others.
- Dr. Theresa Vernetson, Assistant Dean at the University of Florida, always has time to read my work, provide edits, and see things from a point of view that makes any product better.
- SeeLevel Graphics – Matt and Erik are treasures I've found. Their creativity and incredible lens make the final touches seem perfect.
- The Escambia County School District and the Santa Rosa County School District for having faith in the work that Robin and I do by contracting with us for professional development and leadership services. We gain great pleasure working with the leaders and teachers in our respective districts.
- The TeacherReady students, who chose our online alternative pathway to teaching program and have provided us with ways to see the *Student Engagement Framework* in action.
- All the teachers who have participated in the Teachers Teach Students Learn Academies for the past four years in the Escambia County School District. Every summer you give us inspiration to continue working for you.
- Last and certainly not least, I thank and dedicate this book to the many good and passionate teachers in our schools. In particular, I thank several teachers whose work I highlight in *Who's Engaged*. They are outstanding and I sincerely thank them for what they do every day with our students. Thank you –
  - Ms. Atkins
  - Ms. Benjamin
  - Ms. Caddell
  - Ms. Croyle
  - Ms. DeWise
  - Ms. Frite
  - Ms. Hammer
  - Ms. Jones
  - Ms. Russell
  - Ms. Strength
  - Ms. Tow

Table of Contents

INTRODUCTION

In this book I share with you what it takes for students to achieve student learning results when they successfully climb the learning ladder shown in the diagram below. Teachers establish final learning targets or specific measurable learning objectives. Teachers then create daily targets that build on each other to help students take each step up the ladder. As students try to climb the ladder, teachers create ways for students to receive very specific feedback as they are practicing. Teachers and students alike identify student strengths and learning gaps so students can improve their performance. As students continue to move up the ladder they gain more confidence in their learning ability, become more engaged each day, and work hard to achieve the final learning targets.

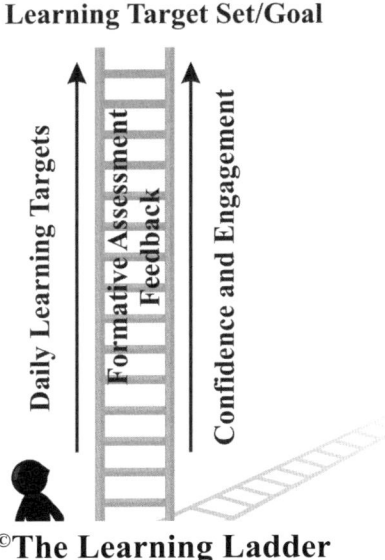

©The Learning Ladder

Anytime students take steps back down the ladder, teachers intervene with new instructional strategies to move them up rather than down. Each step represents a small segment of instruction that helps students achieve the final learning goals. They see how the first step connects to the second step and so on. They also see that if they first tackle step one they will be more likely to make it to step two. Naturally then, moving from step one to step five bypassing the steps in between becomes an illogical and less successful path to take. On the right side of the ladder we see that as students successfully take each step they build confidence and become more engaged learners.

What's the key to getting to the top?

- Aligned learning targets all the way up
- Practice sessions for students to apply their learning
- Coaching from teachers and peers using specific feedback in between steps

By the time you finish reading *Who's Engaged?* you will learn how to develop 30 day and weekly plans to help your students climb the learning ladder, become engaged learners and improve their achievement levels. Part One addresses the "why" to implementing what I call the *Student Engagement Framework* and Part 2 describes the "how" to apply it in your classrooms. Each chapter describes the necessary components to consider when developing 30 day and weekly plans.

Who's Engaged? introduces a practical framework for teachers to use to engage students in the learning process. To illustrate how students become engaged in learning I created the *Student Engagement Framework* (SEF) pictured below. The 30 day and weekly plans set the stage for engaging students to achieve results. For each segment or unit of instruction, students get coached, have time to practice, and receive feedback on specifically aligned and defined learning tasks.

©Student Engagement Framework

Teachers effectively use this framework to help students become more engaged and confident learners, which leads to higher student learning results. When applying the framework, teachers have achieved great success improving student engagement and consequently student learning. Ms. DeWise teaches 2nd grade at a high needs school where 98% of the school's students qualify for free and reduced lunches, which is the district's indicator of poverty. Her students became engaged and all achieved the overall 30 day goal. Enjoy her reflection after she implemented a 30 Day Plan part of the *Student Engagement Framework*.

> *Our curriculum is pretty much laid out for us and with limited time it was difficult to really unpack the benchmark, which I think, now, is a sad situation. Thankfully this training gave me the tools necessary and the knowledge I needed for students to be in charge of their own learning.*
>
> *I started to design my plan by breaking down the process of teaching main idea step by step. Designing the 30-Day plan was time consuming, but it gave me a blueprint of where I was taking my students, how I was going to get them there, and what I was going to do once I got there.*
>
> *In week one, I introduced the daily learning targets to the students before the instruction started to let them know where they were going. I*

wrote the daily learning targets on the board and, each day as a class, we read the daily learning targets before I began the lesson. I wanted the students to know the importance of what we were learning and why.

I began by giving the students a main idea journal, so I could see their work and their daily progress. The first week students focused on defining, recognizing, and drawing pictures about the main idea. I was impressed at how well they did. Out of 15 students 13 students wrote the main idea of pictures without hesitation. Two students had partially correct answers, but with a little feedback from me, they were able to complete the assignment without a problem. I decided to write my own test for the first two weeks because I wanted the test to reflect my learning targets for the week. _15 out of 15 students scored 100% on the test_. I was thrilled on the variety of ways the students conveyed the main idea.

In week two, I again wrote the daily learning targets on the board for everyone to see and every day we read them and practiced them before the lesson started. We focused on defining and recognizing supporting details utilizing pictures. Once they were firm on recognizing details through discussions, students recognized supporting details from a short story that I read. Then the students illustrated the supporting details. After the students practiced for a week, they took the summative assessment that I made. _15 out of 15 students score a 100 % on the test_. I was impressed with my special education students, especially, Makia (pseudonym) who had been performing below grade level but now seemed to be keeping up. Throughout the week students received daily un-graded formative assessments through questioning, discussions and assignments. I then guided my instruction based on the information gained from their assignments.

Before learning about how to apply 30 Day Plans and weekly plans I never thought about giving immediate and specific feedback on anything they did; I just wrote the number of mistakes at the top of the paper and proceeded with the next lesson.

In week three, again, I wrote the daily learning targets on the board and read them every day. One day I forgot to go over the learning targets, but the students reminded me right away. After the students had plenty of practice on finding and highlighting the main idea and supporting details, it was time for them to practice on their own. Students received plenty of practice concerning main idea, and now it was time for them to do it on their own. I read a short story aloud, and then students were placed in groups of three with a cloud graphic organizer. They needed to write the main idea in the cloud and the details in the raindrops. As students worked, I circulated around the room to assess their progress and provide immediate *feedback. During the activity, I saw magical things going on. The students were discussing the story amongst themselves and everyone was engaged in the activity. I enjoyed listening to them carrying on a conversation about main idea and details. One of the students said to the others in the group that the main idea was what the story is mostly about. At the end of the week I assessed my students on locating details from a short paragraph. <u>They did outstanding and the class average was 90%.</u> One of my students who was performing below grade level and who hadn't received a grade higher than a 50 or a 60, scored a 100% on her summative assessment.*

In week four, my students continued to practice. I observed my students' confidence increasing by working together in groups and learning from each other. At the end of the week, students took their summative assessment on main ideas and details with an <u>average of 94%</u>. Again my little Makia scored a 100% on her assessment. We all clapped to celebrate her success. I thought - maybe I finally found a way to teach her so that she can finally experience success.

The *Student Engagement Framework (SEF)* suggests that good teaching seldom occurs without alignment, feedback and evaluation. The tools that help set these three components in motion are 30 day and weekly plans. The outcome is student learning. Viewing the SEF diagram, the first box speaks to alignment. Content standards, daily learning targets communicated to students, and the learning tasks associated with the targets must be aligned. From there, students practice as they receive coaching from their teachers and peers. Valuable coaching includes very specific feedback on strengths of students and identification of learning gaps that occur. The goal is for students to close these gaps and for teachers to create ways for students to receive feedback that does just that. This process is described as using assessment for formative purposes. Once students practice, practice, practice, they are ready to be evaluated to determine their proficiency levels on the learning targets. At this evaluation point, assessments are used for summative rather than formative purposes.

Formative assessment relies on what we do each day to provide feedback to students. Then we know where to begin with them, where students stand as they are trying to learn, how we can help them close their learning gaps, and when students are ready to move to the next learning phase. Specific feedback we provide helps students modify their learning actions from one practice session to another and it moves students closer and closer to hitting the target at a desired level. Teachers applying assessments for formative purposes lead students to achieve higher scores on assessments used for summative purposes.

Students are assessed in a summative nature at some point after students practice learning. Teachers judge how well students achieve on a set of learning targets by using an assessment tool, such as a test or rubric. Put another way, assessments for summative purposes include ways teachers gather student learning data to make a judgment about how well students learned at a particular point in time after students have been coached, practiced learning, and received specific feedback. Teachers assign grades to student results using summative assessment tools; they should not assign grades to any formative assessment data used to help students improve.

Summative assessment tools must be well developed and must accurately measure a subset of learning targets clearly defined by teachers. They include selected response tests or performance assessments of specifically defined learning tasks used for summative purposes - to judge students' performance levels on a set of learning targets.

Often we burden students with too many summative assessment tools to gather information and to record results as part of their grades. This strategy disengages students from learning, which will be discussed in Chapter 2. In contrast, applying the *Student Engagement Framework* directly encourages students to own their learning. Here, we do not have to motivate students to engage; rather, we engage them in learning each day with us and their peers. Teachers who have good teaching skills and the drive to see their students succeed create learning environments where their students thirst to achieve.

Most teachers come to work each day hoping that they can make a difference in their students' lives. To make this happen we need to address each teachers' "what."[1] Ask a teacher to tell you what her "what" is and she'll say - provide me with the best place to work and give me the development I need so that I can be successful. And we know that a teacher's success is judged by her students' success in the classroom. So, teachers must have "will" – desire to improve student learning – and "skill" – tactics to make student learning happen.

You will learn the types of will and skill you need to be effective in your classrooms. The will is driven by the values teachers assume as they walk in and out of their classrooms every day. The skills create better ways for teachers to produce higher student achievement. Teachers must have both will and skill to be effective with students. Good news – most teachers enter the profession because they are value-driven people. So, I leverage teachers' values to introduce how teaching practices need to change to engage students to achieve. Values motivate us and keep us grounded. So, you will find this book motivational and tactical.

I write this book and have published it in an inexpensive way so that many, many teachers can own it to address their "what." Let's face it. Effective teaching does not cost a lot of money and the return on investment for the money spent is invaluable to students. In fact, you will hear me recommend the need for school leaders to reallocate the millions of dollars spent on "silver bullet" programs and products to pay teachers who are committed to learning how to better their skills and refocus their wills. For decades, teachers have witnessed school district leaders spending millions of dollars to buy the "one" content-based program, the "one" curriculum, the "one" data management tool, or the "one" high priced consultant only to find a limited effect on student learning. Just think what might happen if the funds spent on the "one new solution" were spent to pay teachers to help them improve through continuous development practices. Teachers would be more satisfied with their work; students would be more satisfied with their learning; and parents would be more satisfied with their child's education.

In the past four years, my colleague, Dr. Robin Largue, and I have provided professional development for teachers using the *Student Engagement Framework* described in detail in this book. We have received high marks in teacher training sessions focused on the content of this book. On a scale of 1 to 10 with 10 being the highest score we maintain an average rating of 9.80. Why? Because the skills learned get right to the heart of how teachers can improve student learning. A middle school teacher, Ms. Croyle said to me and a group of teachers, "This book is a teacher's gospel – I wish that every teacher and their leaders could read this book." I hope you find it as helpful as she did.

It's my hope that by the time you finish reading this book you will gain or re-kindle your will and a new understanding of the skill needed to help students climb to the top of many learning ladders. *Who's Engaged? Climb the Learning Ladder to See.*

PART ONE
WHY APPLY THE STUDENT ENGAGEMENT FRAMEWORK

Who's Engaged is divided into two parts. The first part addresses 'why' we should use the *Student Engagement Framework*, and the second part focuses on 'how' to apply the framework. Many books and manuscripts focus more on answering the 'what' question. For example, what does it take to create an effective teacher? What should we do to improve reading or math instruction? What types of assessments benefit students? What are the purposes of assessments? These are important questions to answer. However, very few books take the next step and provide teachers and leaders with specific tools needed to improve their practices (Part 2). I believe that for individuals to change their practices they first must understand 'why' they should. Therefore, the first chapters focus on answering 'why' teachers should consider modifying and enhancing the way they teach. Chapter 1 provides an overview of two important studies on effective teaching. Chapters 2 and 3 address how our current practices affect students.

CHAPTER 1
EFFECTIVE TEACHING

Every teacher in every classroom should understand two of the most important research findings discovered in the past several decades. If we understand them, we will work hard to become better and better teachers every day.

In particular, the staggering findings from two important meta-analyses should make us all think twice about our current classroom practices. In the late 90's Paul Black and Dylan Wiliam co-authored the publication, *Inside the Black Box: Raising Standards Through Classroom Assessment*, describing some of the most significant findings in education on student learning.[2] The study focused on one particular aspect of teaching, formative assessment strategies, that occur in classrooms. The findings of their research show that teachers who use formative assessments and provide consistent feedback to students increase student achievement. Assessments used for formative purposes are those that occur as students are learning. Black and Wiliam conducted an extensive survey of the research literature of books and journals over a nine year time period, which yielded about 580 articles or chapters that focused on formative classroom assessment and feedback practices of teachers. Of the 580 manuscripts, they selected 250 to review. They found that students of teachers who used formative assessment practices in their classrooms significantly improved students' performance on standardized tests. The highest gains occurred for lower performing students.

In 1998, Black and Wiliam presented a study that today reinforces how important formative assessment information is to improving student learning. Nine years prior to their study, Royce Sadler wrote a pivotal paper introducing a theory of formative assessment.[3] Sadler identifies three conditions of effective feedback. Students must be able to understand quality work and make good decisions about their work. They, therefore, must be able to compare their work to some sort of standard. Doing so, they can identify their learning gaps and know where they need to improve. Consequently, Sadler proposes that students become more motivated about learning and confident in their abilities.

Sadler suggests that teachers consider using the concept of a feedback loop, which involves teachers and their students simultaneously collecting and analyzing student learning information to determine where students are and where they need to go. Students' progression from one learning target to another works best when students receive descriptive feedback to help them improve. Students rely on feedback and without it, their chance for remaining engaged learners spirals downward.

Similar to the research method Black and Wiliam used when studying formative assessment approaches of teachers, Marzano conducted a meta-analysis to synthesize the research on effective schools.[4] Marzano and his colleagues analyzed research studies that had been conducted over a 35 year time span. They separated the effect of a school's climate on student achievement from the effect an individual teacher had on student achievement. Take a look at the extremely revealing results that provide a strong basis for teachers being the most important variable that affects student learning. Their results revealed the following:

- A student at the 50th percentile who attends an average school and has an average teacher achieves at the 50th percentile and who attends a highly effective school with an average teacher achieves at the 78th percentile.
- The same student at the 50th percentile who attends a least effective school and has an ineffective teacher drops to the 3rd percentile.
- The same student at the 50th percentile who attends a highly effective school and has an ineffective teacher achieves at the 37th percentile.
- The same student at the 50th percentile who attends a highly effective school with a highly effective teacher achieves at the 96th percentile.
- The same student at the 50th percentile who attends a least effective school with a highly effective teacher achieves at the 63rd percentile.

These findings show how important an individual teacher is to student learning. Marzano shows us that highly effective teaching gives schools a greater opportunity to record higher student achievement. Therefore, the teacher affects student achievement more than the school.

These two meta-analyses tell us a great deal about teaching students. The results from Marzano's study shows us that the teacher is the most important variable that affects student learning. The Black and Wiliam study reveals that quality formative assessment practices applied by teachers directly influences student learning with the highest effect on the lowest performing students. These two studies leverage our number one goal as teachers - to improve student learning. We know two important facts from these two studies. First, most students are less likely to achieve without help from a really good teacher. Second, applying a formative assessment process in classrooms provides students with the best opportunities to succeed. In view of that, changing our teaching practices is not a choice for us to make – it is our responsibility.

These two important studies set the stage for what follows. Before we begin, take a moment and reflect on your thinking about your classroom practices by reviewing the statements on the *Effective Teacher GPA Exercise* listed on the next page. Self-reflect on each statement using an A to F grade to rate your performance. Then calculate your GPA. The more honest you are with your ratings, the more open you will be to learn as you read this book. After you complete the self-assessment, read the questions again and assign a letter grade to each item as you answer this question, "How well do you think teachers in general perform the actions?" Then calculate an overall teacher GPA.

- I judge my ability to teach by how well my students learn rather than how well I teach content.
- I am comfortable with others judging my ability to teach by how well my students learn.
- If I leave school knowing many of my students did **not** learn as I expected, I determine that I did **not** teach very well that day.
- I take full responsibility when my students fail to learn.
- I do **not** blame students or their parents for my students failing to learn.
- I do **not** move to another concept until my students have mastered the one at hand.
- Each day I clearly communicate what is expected of my students.
- My students clearly see how one day of learning builds on the next day of learning.
- I give my students ample time to practice learning tasks before I make a judgment about how well they learned.
- I do **not** assign a daily grade to my students' work when they are practicing learning tasks.
- I create opportunities where my students receive continuous and specific feedback that helps them improve.
- I consistently recognize my students' strengths.

At the beginning of a professional development session or a class I ask teachers to take this self-assessment to help us set the stage for learning together. At best, I find teachers tend to assign themselves and other teachers grades that produce a "C" average. Ironically, research over the years tells us that when teachers apply these actions in their classrooms, students achieve higher scores on standardized tests.

Teachers are not altogether responsible for failing to score an "A" on the self-assessment. Teaching my classes and professional development sessions I've found teachers have not been taught strategies that attend to how well students learn rather than what they teach. Good news - when teachers commit to applying the actions above in their classrooms, they regain their passion for teaching.

The information I share, along with some examples of teachers' work, opens doors for teachers to think reflectively about how they need to modify their practices to focus more on what students learn rather than on the content they teach and the activities they do with students each day in class. Teachers can use *Who's Engaged* as a resource to help students climb a learning ladder to achieve academic success.

Sample Effective Teacher GPA Exercise

Self-Assessment	Grade
I judge my ability to teach by how well my students learn rather than how well I teach content.	C
I am comfortable with others judging my ability to teach by how well my students learn.	B
If I leave school knowing many of my students did **not** learn as I expected, I determine that I did **not** teach very well that day.	C
I take full responsibility when my students fail to learn.	B
I do **not** blame students or their parents for my students failing to learn.	B
I do **not** move to another concept until my students have mastered the one at hand.	D
Each day I clearly communicate what is expected of my students.	B
My students clearly see how one day of learning builds on the next day of learning.	C
I give my students ample time to practice learning tasks before I make a judgment about how well they learned.	C
I do **not** assign a daily grade to my students' work when they are practicing learning tasks.	C
I create opportunities where my students receive continuous and specific feedback that helps them improve.	C
I consistently recognize my students' strengths.	B
GPA	**2.33**

©Janet K. Pilcher

CHAPTER 2
—————— STUDENT OWNERSHIP ——————

Third, fourth, and fifth grade teachers at Warrington Elementary School in Pensacola, Florida, collectively put into practice the teaching practices described in this book. In the state of Florida, standardized student test scores are used by the state to "grade" schools. For the last five years, Warrington Elementary School on average received a C grade (one B, three C's, and one D).

Over 80 percent of the students at Warrington are on free or reduced lunches, which is the state's indicator for low socioeconomic student status. Warrington also enrolls a high number of minority and special education students.

In 2008 the school received a "C" grade but the principal, Ms. Peggy Tucker, wanted to do better – she wanted to be an "A" school. She asked us to work with her teachers. We worked intensely with the teachers the summer prior to the last school year (2009) and during the first 30 days of that school year. Our goal was to prepare the teachers to get off on the right foot by creating a plan they applied in the first 30 days of school and carried out during the year.

Three grade level teams (3rd, 4th, and 5th) learned how to apply the *Student Engagement Framework* by creating 30 Day Plans and weekly plans. These plans will be described in more detail in Chapter 8. Noteworthy – the teachers spent time with us to refocus their thinking about how to enter their classrooms each day. They worked hard to shift their thinking about how they judge their effectiveness as teachers. Although admittedly challenging, the teachers stayed focused on what students learned rather than on how well they covered the content. To keep this focus we worked with them to create daily procedures that reinforced students taking ownership of their learning.

The teachers' hard work paid off. At the end of the year, students improved on their standardized tests to gain the school an "A" grade.

The teachers shifted their approach from dictating learning to empowering students to own their learning. Teachers also became owners rather than renters of their professional work. Ms. Tucker, the principal, revealed to us that the beginning of the year started with teachers engaged with each other, solving their own problems, and helping each other become better teachers. Warrington Elementary School became a better place for students to learn, teachers to teach, and parents to engage in their child's education. Opportunities such as this reinforce how lucky our students are to have teachers like those at Warrington Elementary School.

In our own jobs we go to work as "owners" or "renters." And, we have experienced what it is like working with others when their actions say they are "renters" of their work. Renters come to work, do the given tasks of the day, leave when the day ends, and collect their pay for work completed. They look at their evaluation criteria and determine what they need to do to keep their jobs and then adjust their performance to meet the minimum standards that keep them employed. On the other hand, owners in the workplace come to work wanting to make a difference in the organization and in the lives of others. Owners get energy from their peers and customers to do worthwhile work, remain enthusiastic, and commit to do the best job possible. Owners possess a deep sense of pride in their work and exercise reflective practices to constantly improve their performance while simultaneously lifting the performance of the organization. Organizational, professional, and personal goals remain aligned. Owners work as a team to accomplish goals and achieve results. Consequently, owners feel proud of their accomplishments and continue to engage in their work to become stronger and stronger employees.

Do you see differences in students who are renters and owners of their learning? Students who are renters look at an assignment as something assigned to them by the teacher, do the task because it's their job, and expect to receive rewards for their actions or punishments for their inactions. Renters conditionally respond to being told to do the tasks. On the other hand, students as owners of their learning eagerly approach the learning tasks each day and work with other students and the teacher to accomplish the learning goals. Unlike student renters, owners learn without being reminded over and over again.

We live productive and rewarding lives when teaching a class of student owners. So much so, we expect students to enter our classrooms with an "ownership" attitude. When they act as renters, we blame them or their parents for lack of care and concern about learning. Take a quick look in the mirror. We might discover that our teaching practices fail to reinforce students taking ownership of their learning. Do you create learning environments that promote a "do as I say and you will do okay" attitude?

To reinforce this point, let's take a look at the notes Ms. Dunsworth's principal recorded during a classroom observation.

> Ms. Dunsworth is a middle school science teacher. Students enter Ms. Dunsworth's class. She takes roll and then asks them to get out their textbooks. She hands out a worksheet aligned to a specific chapter in the textbook. She asks them to read a book chapter and complete the worksheet. When completed she asks them to place it on the right hand side of their desks. At the end of the class period, she walks around the room to each desk. If the student completed the worksheet, she places a checkmark in the gradebook. If not, she assigns them a checkmark with a minus. Students know that if they complete the worksheet they will adhere to Ms. Dunsworth's directions and receive a positive mark. The focus for these students is on **completing** the task.

Under these learning conditions, students fail to see purpose, understand what and why they are learning, and succumb to or reject to completing what they see as insignificant tasks. Why blame students for failing to participate in an environment remiss of purpose and meaningful work?

As teachers we need to create learning environments that promote student ownership of their learning. In a renter-oriented classroom, teachers focus on what they are teaching and expect students to comply with their directives. Conversely, teachers leading classrooms that reinforce student ownership focus on what students learn each day rather than on what teachers teach. Student ownership then requires that teachers clearly communicate learning targets to students, give students opportunities to practice without being punished, and provide specific feedback to students to help them improve as they get closer and closer to hitting the learning targets. Good formative assessment that promotes student ownership in classrooms depends on students gaining opportunities to practice, receive feedback, and again practice actions that align to clearly delineated learning targets.

Let's revise Ms. Dunsworth's approach to make it better.

> Ms. Dunsworth puts the learning target of the day on the board and explains how this target connects to the previous day's target and how it connects to the big picture of learning. She lets students know that she is going to provide a ten minute instructional segment on the topic at hand. She asks each student to take good notes. Once the ten minute segment is over, she asks each student to answer the following:
>
> • What are the three most important concepts presented?
> • How does each concept connect to something we have previously learned?
> • What more would you like to know to understand the concepts better?
>
> After students take several minutes to complete their responses, she asks students to buddy up with someone to share answers and derive partnered responses. She takes a few minutes at the end of class to ask sets of partners to share their responses to the first question. When students hear others share something on their list, they snap their fingers in unison. This gives Ms. Dunsworth a quick glance on the recorded number of common responses. She collects the responses, collates them after class, and then presents them in a frequency table as an introduction to her lesson at their next class meeting.

Ms. Dunsworth's new approach provides students with opportunities to own their learning. Together, Ms. Dunsworth and her students are engaged with each other in learning. Students realize they are not complying with teacher directives; rather, they naturally follow the sequence of the instruction that involves them. They listen, record, reflect, and engage with others to check their performance.

Prior to teachers applying strategies described in this book, we hear from them that students will not complete an ungraded assignment. Teachers we have worked with changed their thinking when they applied the *Student Engagement Framework*; they deconstructed the standards, developed aligned learning targets, clearly communicated those targets to students, and gave students opportunities to practice while providing specific feedback.

These teachers found most students respond to constructive feedback when it gives them opportunities to improve.

Initially, teachers we have worked with entered their classrooms with lukewarm feelings about how the framework would work. What convinced them? Their students became engaged in their own learning and achieved at A and B levels on the summative assessment tools. Throughout the book I share several examples from teachers' classrooms. For more examples visit *educatorready.com*

CHAPTER 3
STUDENT EMOTIONS

When we receive feedback about our performance from others, it is both an educational and emotional experience. To reap the highest educational benefits, our emotions need to be addressed and understood. Likewise, when students receive information from a teacher about their performance, their self-worth is enhanced or challenged. Students who see possibilities for improving and succeeding continue to work to achieve the goal. Those who constantly experience defeat give up on learning.

I bravely align with the research by promoting that grades fail to serve as a good motivator for student learning, especially for underachieving students. Historically teachers have encouraged unsuccessful learners to act in particular ways by using grades as a punishment tool, such as assigning zeros on incomplete work and taking points off for misbehaving in class. This does little to motivate struggling and unmotivated students to achieve or to improve their behavior. Not all students are motivated by grades, especially those who fall behind on their work and score so low that they see no way out. We've threatened these underachievers with grades enough to know that our punitive actions do not equate to more students succeeding.

Stop for a moment. Take a hard look at the consequences of our actions. Students who face struggles in life, experience constant defeat, and consequently exhibit modest if any confidence enter our doors every day. Many of these students hear us nagging them to complete their work. We threaten to assign an "F" grade. We do this "for the good of students." But students don't necessarily respond to our actions. Naturally, we rationalize their failure by shifting blame from us to them or better yet, their parents. Just when we give up on students, they tease us by turning in their work. Seeing the least amount of effort from underachieving students, we assign them a positive grade on an assignment hoping this grade will motivate them to do more work. Sooner than later students fall into the same old pattern and again receive failing grades from us.

Unlike what we feel about our helping actions, students don't feel good about the effort grade we assigned them. They realize they did not hit the achievement mark. Saying it a little differently, students received something positive from following our directions rather than achieving an academic goal. They don't feel a sense of accomplishment for doing something well. They simply did what we asked them to do. You see, as teachers, our actions with these students follow a long standing myth about grades motivating students. This myth has lingered with us way too long. It's time to put it to bed.

Students emotionally experience assessments. We are responsible for knowing where, when and how these emotions occur during the instructional process. Rick Stiggins shares an assessment experience chart describing what "winning" and "losing" streaks look like for students in our classrooms.[5] I suggest that students on the losing side have not consistently experienced a classroom where teachers clearly communicate well defined learning targets and use good formative assessment approaches to coach students to succeed. Stiggins shares that students who are on the losing side possess all or some of the following characteristics:

- continuously see evidence of failure,
- feel like nothing works,
- receive feedback from teachers in the form of criticism,
- feel hurt and embarrassed,
- seek learning environments that are easy,
- give up when challenged,
- experience one defeat after another,
- do not always complete work for fear of failure, and
- see no relevance and purpose to assigned tasks by the teacher.

As teachers, our goal is to place students in winning situations where they are eager to learn, take on challenges, and own their learning. We need to enter our classrooms each day with one purpose in mind that comes from Coach John Wooden, one of the best basketball coaches and teachers of all time. To be effective teachers, he tells us "we have not taught students, until they have learned."[6] We shouldn't judge our effectiveness by how much we teach, what we teach, and how we teach. Rather, we make a positive judgment if we've approached students every day knowing that our success depends on how well students learn. I suggest that applying the *Student Engagement Framework* helps us make this shift in our thinking. We must judge our work as teachers by viewing how well students learned, especially students who struggle the most.

Providing students with very specific feedback on what they do well and where they need to improve is an essential part of the *Student Engagement Framework*. Following Black and Wiliam's study, I suggest teachers help students climb a learning ladder to success. Doing so requires teachers to make a culture shift in the way they think about planning and teaching. Our job as teachers is to plan and teach with one purpose in mind – to engage students to perform at their highest potential. Before we learn how to carry out this purpose, let's talk more about how to view student performance and student engagement.

Students emotionally experience assessments. We are responsible for knowing where, when and how these emotions occur during the instructional process.

The Studer Group has studied hundreds of healthcare organizations and found employees fall into three major performance categories: high, middle and low. About 92 % of employees move in and out of middle to high performing behaviors when presented with new information and performance tasks. The other 8% do one of three things - change their behavior to become better employees, self-select out of the organization, or are removed from their jobs by their leaders. Studer Group found when leaders uniformly apply leadership best practices, only one to three percent of employees refuse to change their behaviors.

Perhaps we can apply this high, middle, and low performer concept to students in our classrooms. With good coaching by teachers, the majority of students will move up the performance ladder. When teachers clearly communicate learning targets, model quality performance and apply formative assessment strategies during the practice sessions, students identify learning gaps, improve their performance, and gain a winning momentum. The feeling of success inspires students to engage in learning each day. Almost all students become engaged and improved learners. Only one to three percent may decide not to perform or face extreme barriers to learning. These students' behaviors or learning difficulties should be handled at a school level by a school leader. Look closely at what this means. – in a group of 50 students only one or two students will flat out refuse to engage in learning if the teacher uses strategies that engage students.

So, what do we consider when moving student performance up? Quint Studer describes four phases of learning something new which are presented in Figure 3.1 - unconsciously unskilled, consciously unskilled, consciously skilled, and unconsciously skilled.[7] Let's look at how these four phases play out with students in our classrooms. Students enter our classrooms at the beginning of the year unconsciously unskilled. Students are excited, eager to learn, and ready for a new year. After several weeks into the semester they become consciously unskilled. They experience feedback on their work from teachers that causes some type of pain or stress. They begin wondering if they will succeed and if achieving is worth their effort.

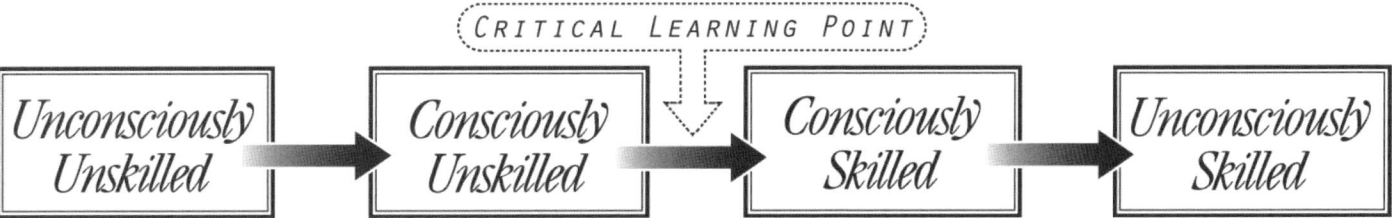

Figure 3.1 Competent Phases
©Studer Group

To help us better understand what these students experience let's review the concept of creative tension introduced by Peter Senge in his book, *The Fifth Discipline*.[8] Creative tension is a gap between what is comfortable and uncomfortable when we realize that moving to the goal means doing something that is unfamiliar to us. He tells us this gap creates a type of energy. The emotions that arise from this gap – worry, discouragement, hopelessness – can be redirected when we focus on the goal and align our actions to that goal. When this focus does not occur, we may choose to lower our expectations to reduce anxiety. Also, we may choose to give up, blame others, or wait for this event to be over to get back to business as usual. Students constantly experience creative tension as each new concept is presented by the teacher. Teachers' interactions with students at the critical learning point (consciously unskilled to consciously skilled) determine if students achieve the learning targets at desired levels, students lower their expectations, or students decide to remain consciously unskilled.

When students experience emotional tension as they try to make the shift from the consciously unskilled to the consciously skilled phase, teachers must create ways for students to practice and receive pointed feedback that identifies gaps and reinforces strengths. The best learning occurs at the point the tension rises if and only if descriptive feedback blended with encouragement takes place. At this point more than any other, if teachers use assessments in punitive ways students begin sliding into the losing streak that Rick Stiggins talks about. Students begin stepping down the learning ladder. Some become disengaged, others become discipline problems. A few students do what they naturally do. They get frustrated with the chaotic environment and comply with the requirements as a way to get by or out of the classroom as soon as possible. Parents of these students may choose to remove their child in favor of another classroom or school, if available and allowable.

Coaching students at this most tense moment determines effective or ineffective teaching. Even teachers who have had successful student learning results could get even better results by paying attention to those moments where tension in learning occurs or what I call the *critical learning point*.

A teacher's ability and willingness to coach students and associate student success with how well students learn rather than what they teach becomes extremely critical to move students from consciously unskilled to consciously skilled. At this critical learning point, students depend on teachers helping, not hurting them. Students become consciously skilled when they see clearly defined learning targets, when learning tasks are connected with those targets, and when they receive specific feedback as they practice moving from target to target.

As students gain confidence by successfully climbing up the steps of the learning ladder they begin owning rather than renting their learning. They shift from being teacher dependent to self-directed learners. Students get to the competent phases when they engage in the learning process every day studying feedback about their performance during practice sessions. At the last phase, unconsciously skilled, students learn the task so well they are able to perform at high levels again and again, transfer the learned skills to other learning situations, and perform well on standardized tests. Consequently, teachers spend less time during the year on test preparation. That is, when test time comes students are prepared – they've practiced applying important skill sets time and again in their classrooms.

The movement through these four phases shows us how students emotionally experience assessments. Students receive specific feedback needed to move them from one learning target to another, one day at a time until they achieve a set of learning targets with recognized competence. As they experience success by achieving one learning target at a time, students gain confidence in their abilities. They feel better about themselves. Accordingly, they get a natural high by becoming engaged learners.

CLASSROOM STUDENT ENGAGEMENT

Our goal as teachers is to create learning environments where students want to learn and gain confidence as they experience success. For this to occur, teachers need to know what each student wants from them. Students want teachers who visibly

- care about them;
- engage them in the learning process;
- recognize them for the step-by-step progress made;
- believe they can learn;
- like being with them in the classroom; and
- teach them as individuals.

To be that type of teacher we must walk out of our classrooms every day judging our success by how well students learn. Common sense if nothing else tells us engaged students will improve their performance in our classrooms. To help us gauge our success I created the *Classroom Student Engagement Scale* as a way to check the level of student engagement in our classrooms. Explicitly, the questions on the *Classroom Student Engagement Scale* I created focus on how students feel about their learning in class with their teacher.

Take a moment to reflect on your current practices. Review the questions on the *Classroom Student Engagement Scale* in Figure 3.2. How well do you engage your students? Using a 1 to 5 rating scale with "5" representing always and "1" representing never, how would your students rate the items?

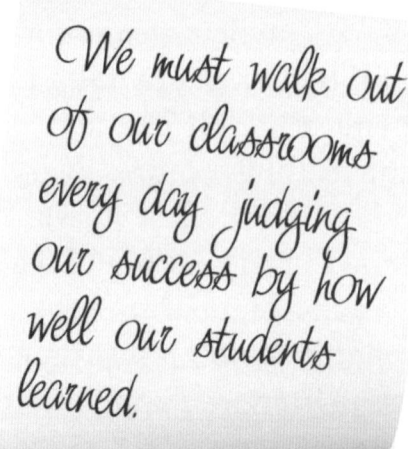

Are we providing students with what they want from us? Are they engaged? Most of us see that we can do better. The *Classroom Student Engagement Scale* provides a way for us to "check" ourselves on how what we are doing engages or disengages students. Here are some ways to use the scale:

- At end of each week or two, thinking of the entire class, determine how you think the class as a whole would answer the questions.
- Answer the questions three different times - once thinking about a high achieving student, once thinking about an average student, and once thinking about a low achieving student
- If you get a wild hair, ask your students how they would respond. Then compare their responses to your perceptions.

The defined *Student Engagement Framework* I describe in the remaining chapters of this book gives us the framework and the tools we need to engage our students each day they walk through our classroom doors. At the end of the day, we ask ourselves the question that Coach Wooden asked himself time and again, "Today, did our students learn?" If the answer is yes, we know we taught well. If the answer is no, we use student assessment data to modify and improve our instruction so that students learn well the next day. If the answer is for some students 'yes' and for others 'no,' we create strategies to help those students in need and recognize those who have achieved. Remember Makia, Ms. DeWise's second grade student, who overcame great obstacles to achieve after receiving help from her teacher and her classmates. The end result – she hit the learning target and her classmates cheered.

Scale:
5 Always
4 Almost Always
3 Sometimes
2 Seldom
1 Never

	Classroom Student Engagement Scale	1	2	3	4	5
1	I know what the learning expectations are in my classroom.	1	2	3	4	5
2	I have the materials I need to achieve the daily learning targets.	1	2	3	4	5
3	In class I know what I need to do to improve.	1	2	3	4	5
4	I am rewarded and recognized for successful work.	1	2	3	4	5
5	My teacher seems to care about me as a person.	1	2	3	4	5
6	I am encouraged by others in my classroom to improve each day.	1	2	3	4	5
7	I am comfortable demonstrating my work to others.	1	2	3	4	5
8	Our goals in class make me feel the work I do is important.	1	2	3	4	5
9	My classmates come to class each day wanting to complete quality work.	1	2	3	4	5
10	I feel comfortable turning to other students to help me succeed.	1	2	3	4	5
11	My teacher talks to me about my progress on a regular basis.	1	2	3	4	5
12	I come to class each day wanting to learn.	1	2	3	4	5
13	My teacher helps me overcome obstacles that keep me from learning.	1	2	3	4	5
14	I enjoy coming to class.	1	2	3	4	5
15	My teacher believes I can be a successful learner.	1	2	3	4	5
16	If I don't succeed the first time my teacher encourages me to try again.	1	2	3	4	5

Figure 3.2 Classroom Student Engagement Scale
©Janet K. Pilcher

PART TWO
HOW TO APPLY THE STUDENT ENGAGEMENT FRAMEWORK

We work in a values-driven profession. When we learn and apply a best practice that leads to improved student learning our values kick in. Put another way, our values will not let us continue to do "old" things in our classrooms that potentially harm our students or not do "new" things that provide our students with best opportunities for achieving success. The *Student Engagement Framework* speaks to teachers' values. Therefore, I developed processes and tools associated with the framework that teachers can use to reinforce student learning. From my work with teachers I realize that some haven't been taught the essential skills needed to become effective teachers, or leaders have failed to continue to reinforce the skills with their teachers.

Chapters 4 to 8 focus on how to apply each part of the *Student Engagement Framework* to connect back to the 'why' presented in Chapters 1 to 3. Chapters 4 and 5 focus on the first box of the framework describing how to align learning targets to learning tasks. Chapter 6 provides some specific tools teachers can use to provide feedback to students as they are learning. Chapter 7 summarizes summative assessment guidelines for developing good assessment tools. Chapter 8 describes how to combine the "how tos" to create 30 day and weekly plans and provides some examples from teachers.

CHAPTER 4
LEARNING TARGETS

For students to learn they need to know what is expected of them. Therefore, teachers must create and effectively communicate clearly defined learning targets. These targets need to be posted in the same place in the classroom every day. With the learning targets posted, students know the expectations as soon as they enter class.

Learning targets guide teachers on what they are to teach and students on what they are to learn. Therefore, we want to write them in clear and measurable ways. How? Learning targets must contain a capability verb similar to those listed in Figure 4.1 and an action a student will do. The verb indicates the skill level of the performance the student will demonstrate and describes the skill that will be directly observed. Sometimes the capability verbs 'know' and 'understand' are included in a taxonomy chart. I do not recommend using these two verbs. We cannot determine when a student 'knows or understands' something nor visually see what 'know' and 'understand' look like. Conversely, when a student 'states,' 'identifies', and 'sorts' things, we clearly appreciate how this looks in action. The verb helps us visually see the type of performance we are looking for.

Mental Levels	Sample Measurable Capability Verbs
Knowledge	arrange, define, duplicate, label, list, memorize, name, order, recognize, relate, recall, repeat, reproduce, state, sort
Comprehension	classify, describe, discuss, explain, express, identify, indicate, locate, recognize, report, restate, review, select, translate
Application	apply, choose, demonstrate, dramatize, employ, illustrate, interpret, operate, practice, schedule, sketch, solve
Analysis	analyze, appraise, calculate, categorize, compare, contrast, criticize, differentiate, discriminate, distinguish, examine, experiment, question, test
Synthesis	arrange, assemble, collect, compose, construct, create, design, develop, formulate, manage, organize, plan, prepare, propose
Evaluation	appraise, argue, assess, attach, choose, defend, estimate, judge, predict, rate, select, support, value, evaluate

Figure 4.1 Bloom's Taxonomy and Sample Measurable Verbs[9]

A student action follows a verb. An action is the "thing" students do to demonstrate their ability to apply the desired knowledge or skill associated with the mental levels of Bloom's Taxonomy. Some examples of well written learning targets that include a capability verb for each mental level are:

Mental Level	Learning Targets
Knowledge	List (capability verb) the steps of the scientific method (action).
Comprehension	Locate (capability verb) the capitals of the U.S. states on the map (action).
Application	Illustrate (capability verb) the main idea and supporting details of the story using a mind map (action).
Analysis	Compare (capability verb) two interviews presented by two different reporters (action).
Synthesis	Create (capability verb) a podcast to tell the story of a given novel (action).
Evaluation	Argue (capability verb) for a point of view provided to you on a critical issue (action).

A number of scholars have created taxonomies that include capability verbs and mental level categories. The taxonomies, similar to the one presented in Figure 4.1 begin at the knowledge level of learning and move to complex skills. The capability verbs attached to each level provide visible descriptions of what we should recognize when we observe student learning.

One word of caution. We need to make sure we select verbs that connect to the complexity level of the skill we ask students to demonstrate. For example, let's discuss a common learning target, "identify the main idea of a given passage." This is a very complicated skill that is not represented by the verb, identify. A better learning target for the skill at hand is "analyze the language in the written passage to identify the main idea." The point here is not to get caught up on the language used but to think about both the skill being assessed and the complexity level of that skill. Detailed scaffolding (breaking down learning targets into very specific skills) needs to occur in the instructional process for students to achieve more complex skills. Let's look at an example of scaffolding for the skill, *analyze a passage to identify main idea*, noting how the learning targets build from lower to higher complexity levels.

• Define main idea.
• Describe what it means to select the main idea in a passage.
• Given a passage with the selected main idea, explain why the selection is the main idea.

- Given 3 different passages and underlined statements representing main ideas within each paragraph, select the correct main idea.
- Given a passage, analyze the text and identify the main idea

The verbs become handy tools for us to use as we scaffold learning. Think of students climbing a learning ladder. For each segment or unit of instruction, they move from one learning target to another attempting to get to the top of the ladder. We scaffold instruction well when we align learning tasks to the targets and provide descriptive feedback while students practice the tasks. Our actions enable students to achieve the essential learning goals at the top of the learning ladder associated with a particular instructional segment. Let's learn more.

SCAFFOLDS OF LEARNING TARGETS

As we see from the examples and the capability verbs in the chart, students need to know how to master successfully the learning targets that serve as prerequisite knowledge to other targets. Remember the learning ladder diagram. Students climb one step at a time. To get to the top they have to achieve the targets that support a step by step movement up the ladder.

Learning Target Set/Goal

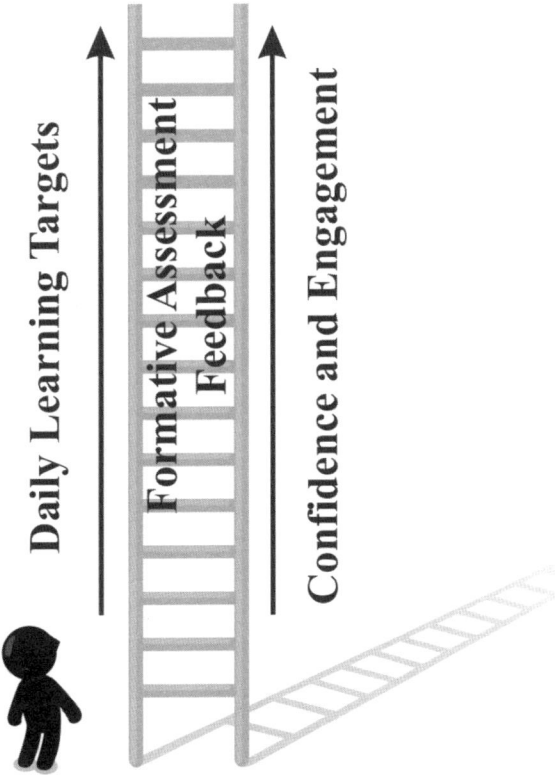

The Learning Ladder

Let's look at a typical example that fails to represent good teaching practices. The skill that requires students to "compare" something is a fairly complex skill. Let's say that we are studying the fall of the stock market over a six month period. We want students to compare the stories of two CNN reporters. Students first need to learn the prerequisite content about stock markets prior to applying a more complex skill, compare. As teachers we should create learning targets that build on each other to teach the content to help students grasp that necessary knowledge needed to apply the complex skill of comparing two news stories.

Unlike the approach just described we find a typical teacher's approach similar to Mr. Burt's. Mr. Burt, a high school economics teacher, asks students to read a chapter in their textbooks on stock markets. He then gives students a set of questions to answer as they review graphs from the local business section of the newspaper and the content in the chapter they've read. Immediately following, Mr. Burt shows two CNN reporting segments and asks students to write several paragraphs that compare the two interviews presented. His students do not see learning targets nor do they have opportunities to practice prerequisite skills they need to achieve the overall goal. The point – students are unclear of the learning expectations and struggle to find relevance in this activity.

Before students are able to apply a skill, they must have knowledge of the content. Mr. Burt attempted to provide the knowledge necessary by asking students to complete questions using the stock market graphs. He thought by giving the students this activity, they would be able to apply what they learned from the graphs to understand the main points of the CNN news reporter clips. Two problems exist. First, students cannot automatically make connections from content to application without the learning expectations being clearly defined. Second, many students cannot apply a complex skill without first acquiring the prerequisite knowledge and skills needed to do so.

Consequently, some students get frustrated and give up, some get bored and quit, others complete the task without a deep understanding, and a few students are able to connect the dots on their own to complete the task without needing much assistance.

What's a better way for Mr. Burt to help students learn? Once students have a general knowledge level of stock markets this knowledge can be expanded when students apply complex skills. To achieve the complex task, "compare two interviews," students need to acquire an understanding for applying the "compare" skill well. We do just that when we create a scaffold of learning targets such as:

• Recall the major points of the two stories presented by two reporters.
• Restate the major points of the two stories in your own language.

• Explain the significance of the two points of view to the topic at hand.
• Sketch a diagram that associates like points to each other.
• Compare the two interviews presented by two different reporters.

For every major skill set we want students to learn, we must think about what students need to know first, second, third, and so on until they finally achieve the most complex skill expected. If we want students to think critically we must teach them how. Scaffolding learning by connecting every dot does just that.

Mr. Burt's new targets move from the most basic, knowledge level, to higher cognitive levels in *Bloom's Taxonomy*. Specifically, "recall" and "restate" are learning targets written at the knowledge level. The next targets that ask students to "explain" and "sketch" something prepare them to first comprehend and then apply knowledge. The final skill, "compare," is the most complicated of this instructional segment.

Teachers take the first step to engage students to learn when they create learning targets that scaffold instruction and when they consistently communicate targets each day. The outcome is higher student achievement.

A COMMUNICATION TOOL

Learning targets written in very clear and simple terms provide us with a way to communicate learning expectations to students every day. Students see the bigger learning goal and how the smaller targets guide them to achieve the ultimate goal, to climb to the top of the ladder. Listen to Ms. Benjamin's reflection about communicating targets to students. She changed her practice and began writing the daily learning target on the board.

> *I listened to the "buzz." (after all we are known as Benjamin's Busy Bees). The students were reading, "Recognize setting and characters in a story." They began to talk among themselves about what recognize meant, then the discussion turned to setting and finally characters. There was speculation all around the room. As I heard their excitement and curiosity mount, I was anxious to begin. They settled down to begin their morning work and I proceeded to take care of attendance, lunch count, etc.*

> *At 8:45, I proceeded to the front of the classroom and read the target, asking several students to explain what it meant. After several responses, I clarified any confusion and assigned reading partners, a higher level reader with a struggling reader. They went off to read the story, hunting for the setting and characters, armed*

with their reading book, reading log and a pencil. I circulated around the room, taking notes.

Each day, I added the daily target and listened to the discussions. The students began to look forward to what would be on the board each day. One student said that it was like finding clues to a mystery they were trying to solve. I thought that was a perfect analogy. By the end of the first week, the students were "hooked" and so was I. Why I hadn't been more specific with my learning targets (objectives) before, is beyond me. I saw improvement in students' interaction with the text. They were definitely more engaged in the reading process.

Ms. Russell teaches a special education class and started her class by writing the learning targets on the board and talking about what they meant. Below she describes her students' view of the change in her practices. The comments are from a group of special education students who have struggled to perform well on the state standardized test. Hear what her students had to say.

I asked the students how they liked our new lesson plans and they all said to some extent: We don't have to ask what we are doing anymore. We already know. We know what we need to bring to group and everything. It makes it easy Ms. Russell.

I've heard some teachers say that if the learning targets get erased from the board the students call the teacher's attention to the missing item. What do learning targets do for teachers and students? It lets students know why they are learning, aligns instruction to the goals, and keeps everyone focused on what is to be achieved. Well developed and communicated learning targets that build on one another lay the groundwork for effective teaching.

An important note. When students first learn a new skill, they need for teachers to carefully scaffold instruction without missing important steps. In other words, students need to **slowly** climb one step at a time on the learning ladder. Once the foundational skills are learned, students quickly progress up the first steps of the ladder to get to the more complicated skills. For these learned foundational skill sets, students become unconsciously skilled. For these students, teachers begin their instruction at more complex levels. Remember, however, if certain students fall behind or get frustrated, check their achievement level on the lower steps of the learning ladder and re-teach those skills to those students.

CHAPTER 5
LEARNING TASKS

As we scaffold learning up the learning ladder, we must consider how learning tasks connect to learning targets. The connection helps students see how their actions in class help them achieve one learning target at a time knowing at every moment they are moving to that final learning goal. If we, as teachers, can't see that connection, we surely know our students can't either.

A learning task is the action students complete to produce learning data that can be used to assess student progress. Students must see how these tasks align to the targets. As teachers we may spend a considerable amount of time on learning tasks associated with each learning target helping students climb up each step on the learning ladder to achieve the final goal. A key point – we only move to the next learning target when students achieve the subsequent one. Climbing each step, students witness clear learning expectations, practice learning tasks with others, and receive feedback on what they do well and where they need to improve.

What do we consider as we scaffold learning targets and align them to learning tasks? First, we communicate each learning target and its relevance to the final goal. Ms. Strength, a first grade teacher, says it best, "Aligned and connected learning targets create a map to a treasure chest for students to learn." Students know where they are, what they need to do, and where they need to go. Therefore, our goal, as teachers, is to communicate learning targets students use to navigate their learning.

Second, to give students a snapshot of quality, we explain and demonstrate what good performance represents so that students know what they are trying to achieve. Jan Chappius suggests that when teachers teach a skill using examples and non examples of work samples they provide students with a visual of where to go and importantly, where not to go.[10] Sometimes we learn what to do when we know what not to do.

Third, to help students improve, students and teachers collect student learning information using feedback strategies during practice sessions. Sometimes a measure associated with each target helps us determine student achievement levels. For example, let's say we are working on the target, "recall the major points of two stories." At the end of our practice session, we may give students five situations and ask them to demonstrate their competence on the "recall" target. We set a four out of five measure as the expected achievement level before moving to the next target. Once we get a performance check on the learning target using our preset measure, we know how well students have mastered the skill at hand and if not, how we might re-teach the skill to help them get closer to the learning target.

Remember, Mr. Burt. He asked these questions to determine how to make changes to his instruction: What learning tasks would help students master the target? How will these learning tasks assist students in achieving the targets? How prepared would students be to move to the next target? How will these learning tasks help students learn the prerequisite knowledge and skills to reach the final target?

Recall he wanted students to be able to "compare two interviews." For students to achieve this skill, he first created learning targets that helped him scaffold instruction.

- Recall the major points of the two stories presented by the reporters.
- Restate information in their own language.
- Explain the significance of the two points of view.
- Sketch a diagram associating similar points.
- Compare the two interviews.

To engage students he realized he needed to teach students how to apply the prerequisite skills prior to expecting them to compare information. Before he made a final decision about how well students compared the two interviews, he understood students must clearly realize what it takes for them to achieve each learning target.

Let's look in more detail at how he engaged students when addressing the first learning target, "recall the major points of the two stories presented by two reporters." He gets students ready for the day by writing the recall learning target on the board and engaging in a discussion with his students about the target. He explains how this target is the first in a sequence of targets to help students achieve the final learning goal that is also posted on the board. He then proceeds with the following actions:

1. To refresh students' memory, Mr. Burt provides about 5 to 7 minutes of instruction on main ideas and supporting details.

2. Mr. Burt shows the clip of the first reporter. He asks students to jot down what they believe to be the main points of the reporters' viewpoint.

3. Mr. Burt asks students to get into their previously assigned groups of four, and he assigns a group leader for the day.

4. In their groups, Mr. Burt asks students to discuss what they believe to be the main points and to record those points on the post-it-note chart paper pad.

5. He asks two group leaders to place their groups' sheets of paper on the recording wall.

6. He then asks all groups to talk about how their items compare with the two groups' posted work. They have different color dots assigned to each group. After a 3 minute discussion, the group leaders place dots on all items their groups believe to be the the main points using all group data on the wall. Mr. Burt has posted an empty sheet. If after reviewing the groups' information, a group believes a point has been missed by all groups, the group leader places that point on the empty sheet. Dots can also be placed on the points presented on that sheet.

7. Mr. Burt provides a chart to students for them to complete.

Main Points Presented	# of dots	Agree that it is a main point	Disagree it is a main point
		AGREE	DISAGREE
		AGREE	DISAGREE
		AGREE	DISAGREE
		AGREE	DISAGREE
		AGREE	DISAGREE
		AGREE	DISAGREE
		AGREE	DISAGREE

8. Mr. Burt places the main points of the reporters on the white board and asks students to check to see how well they did. If students missed main points altogether, he provides that information to students and asks them to add it to their charts. He then enters into a discussion trying to close any gaps of students who missed the main points. If needed he reintroduces the difference between main points and supporting details. He uses the data in the charts to help make this point.

9. Mr. Burt shows the clip of the second reporter and works with students to complete the same steps 1 to 8 above.

10. He then asks students to turn in their charts. On the top left hand corner he asks them to write the word, green (meaning 'got it'), yellow (meaning 'getting there'), or red (meaning "didn't get it').

The first seven steps represent the learning tasks that serve as a way to collect data about student learning. Numbers 8 and 10 represent formative assessment strategies Mr. Burt used to get a sense of how well students did on the learning target at hand. Important – the learning task is the action students do as they are learning. The formative assessment strategy is the way students present data so that others can see how well they achieved and where learning gaps exist. To reinforce the recall target, Mr. Burt moves to the next target asking students to restate the main points in their own language. As a learning task he may ask them to write a summary paragraph that provides an overview of the main points of both CNN reporters' viewpoints. At this step, Mr. Burt collects data to assess how well students identified the main points and how well they communicated those points in writing. He will have to make sure students understand the expectations for both parts of the learning task. Here, he could refresh their memories by providing an example and non example of a good summary paragraph. All the while, Mr. Burt is working with students and students are working with each other to achieve the final learning goal - for students to compare the two interviews. To do so, he works with students to achieve one learning goal at a time.

We create learning targets that build on each other so that students can clearly see how one learning step connects to another. Students see how accomplishing one target helps them accomplish the next and the next until finally they have accomplished the final learning goal. As students practice the learning tasks and receive descriptive feedback, the information is used by teachers and students to determine where students are and how they need to improve.

ENOUGH TIME

Around this point in professional development sessions with teachers they ask, "with all we have to do, how will we have time to put the *Student Engagement Framework* in action?" Teachers worry about having enough time to do the work needed to engage students. Maybe a better question is do we make efficient use of the time we have? To learn more about how we spend our time complete the time exercise.

Time Exercise	
Where do you spend your time each week	**Hours Per Week**
1. How many hours per week do you spend doing unproductive planning? (using a process that does not include well developed and communicated learning targets, aligned instruction to targets, specific feedback to students, and development of good summative assessment tools)	
2. How many hours per week do you spend responding to poorly communicated mandates?	
3. How many hours per week do you spend dealing with disruptive students or discipline problems?	
4. How many hours per week do you spend communicating negative information to students?	
5. How many hours per week do you spend communicating negative information to parents?	
Add these hours	
1. How many hours per week do you spend doing productive planning?	
2. How many hours a week do you spend on rewarding and recognizing students?	
3. How many hours per week do you spend sending a positive note or making a positive phone call home to parents?	
4. How many hours per week do you spend coaching students to learn by using specific formative assessment strategies?	
5. How many hours a week do you spend using student learning data to reflect on and modify your instruction?	
Add these hours	

©Janet K. Pilcher (modified from Studer Group's time exercise with leaders)

Do you spend more hours per week on the first set of questions? Over the years most of us have spent more hours on items at the top of the chart than on the bottom. Applying the *Student Engagement Framework* helps us spend our time on actions listed on the bottom of the chart.

Gaining new skills will allow teachers to reallocate time to students' learning and away from discipline problems that plague them each day. I've found that teachers may lack some essential skills that cause them to lose instructional time, or they lack the drive to make more efficient use of time. Teachers tell us that when they apply the *Student Engagement Framework* they save time in the long run.

More and more teachers say that they are given more mandates with less time to plan and teach. In particular, states and districts send the "coverage" message. Teachers are required to cover all the content standards, which sometimes number more than teaching days allotted during a school year. Teachers say things like "If we re-teach unlearned skills and focus on in-depth student learning, we will not have enough time to cover all the standards."

I'm a believer that when we pose a problem, we must come forward with a solution. So, here it is. For this discussion let's speak about those standards most tested - writing, reading, and mathematics. Within each of these content areas, wouldn't you agree that very specific, common skill sets are required of students to be successful at being a good writer, reader or mathematician? And, don't these skills scatter across grade levels but at varying levels of complexity? As we teach content on different topics our underlying focus then should be on teaching and reinforcing these very defined and important skill sets. All of us can wrap our minds around this strategy.

Also, no matter the content area (science, history, the arts) students work to apply common complex skills to solve problems. For example, skills such as compare, contrast, analyze, design, and evaluate scatter across academic areas. As teachers in various content areas we may decide to focus simultaneously on a common complex skill (sometimes referred to as a critical thinking skill) for a 30 day time period so that students can transfer a particular skill to all content areas. For students to master the complex skill we must scaffold the instruction well in each of our content areas. Most students can't reach higher learning levels without our help. We don't necessarily teach critical thinking skills; rather, critical thinking occurs as we purposefully scaffold learning. It's not that some can critically think and others cannot. Most all students can achieve complex skills if we teach them how. It just takes some students a little more practice than others.

As teachers, if we are serious about all students learning, we must gain the best skills needed to improve the way we spend our time. At the end of the day every teacher leaving school should answer this question positively: "Have all my students learned well?" Our work and the findings of important studies show that students learn when teachers use strategies that engage students. No excuses - tackling time becomes our responsibility.

With that said, we can't ignore educational systems' failure to give teachers enough time to improve their practices, plan for instruction, and reflect on daily student feedback. Systemic changes addressing these two arguments are beyond the scope and purpose of this book. However, we hope that leaders and policy-makers read the information presented here and in *How To Lead Teachers to Become Great*[11] and let the content sit in the forefront of any educational reform initiative. We present results-driven approaches on how teachers become highly effective, which is judged by engaged student learning and achievement.

Our work is with teachers and students in classrooms. Here, educational reform begins as an important grassroots effort starting with what it takes to have students in classrooms led by highly effective teachers. We, as teachers, need to promote this grassroots reform position. To do so, we must first apply measurable practices that yield engaged and improved learners. Consequently, classroom student learning results will gain credibility and hold value to others making judgments about how well students learned.

To the dislike of many teachers, for decades standardized student achievement has sat in the driver's seat of education reform and accountability. Our work and results with teachers suggest that higher standardized test scores take a more appropriate place by becoming an upshot of educational change that happens in our classrooms.

CHAPTER 6
PRACTICE AND FEEDBACK

Learning makes more sense to students when they experience learning tasks that specifically connect to learning targets communicated by teachers. Likewise, feedback strategies coexist alongside student assignments and function as part of the instructional process. We naturally give students feedback as they complete learning tasks. Feedback strategies allow us to create formal ways to give students timely feedback. Also, students gain feedback from themselves and other students. Information we gather from the feedback strategies determines if we need to modify our instruction for the next day's lesson or continue on.

We informally assess student progress each day. We look at body language and expressions, listen to the types of questions students ask, and analyze students' frustration levels. These informal formative strategies are important. However, they do not directly involve students in reflecting about their own performance, making learning connections, and taking ownership of their learning. We need some tools to help us do just that.

The tools described in this chapter equip teachers and their students with methods for taking learning "pulse checks." As students climb from one step to the next they need a quick check on how they are doing. Simple tools provide helpful information at critical times during the learning process (the critical learning point described in Chapter 3). Keep six rules of thumb in mind that explain why we should provide descriptive feedback and coach students to learn.

SIX RULES OF THUMB

First, provide feedback to recognize good performance. We often express what students do wrong, but seldom reward and recognize good performance. Similar to most all of us, students respond when they are recognized. Using research findings from Gallup's work on employee engagement[12], Studer speaks to the 3 to 1 compliment principle.

$\dfrac{3 \text{ Compliments}}{1 \text{ Criticism}} = \begin{matrix}\text{Positive} \\ \text{Behavior}\end{matrix} \qquad \dfrac{2 \text{ Compliments}}{1 \text{ Criticism}} = \begin{matrix}\text{Neutral} \\ \text{Behavior}\end{matrix} \qquad \dfrac{1 \text{ Compliments}}{1 \text{ Criticism}} = \begin{matrix}\text{Negative} \\ \text{Behavior}\end{matrix}$

Here are some suggestions on ways to recognize and reward students.

- Send a thank you note to students expressing your appreciation for a specific performance or behavior that deserves to be recognized.

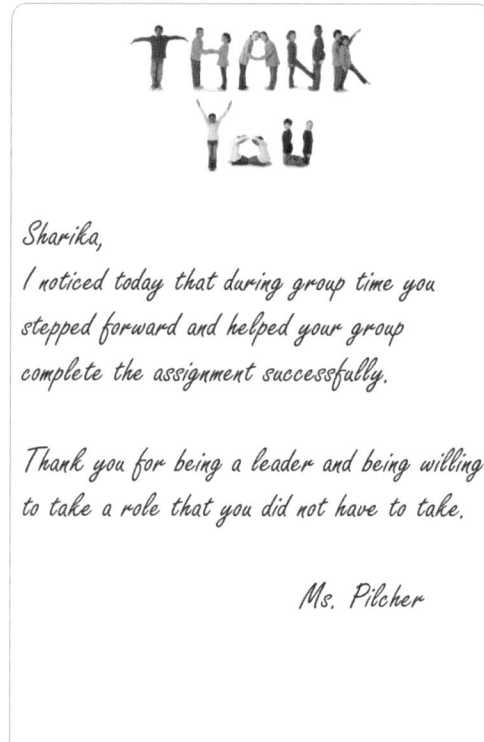

Sharika,
I noticed today that during group time you stepped forward and helped your group complete the assignment successfully.

Thank you for being a leader and being willing to take a role that you did not have to take.

Ms. Pilcher

- Create a class recognition board and place shining stars with the students' names and the recognized performances or behaviors. In the example below, a digital picture of Olivia was cut into the shape of a star. The specific performance achieved is written underneath his picture. What a win for Olivia! Send it to her parents and get another win.

Olivia solved 4 out of 5 word problems correctly!

• Phone or send notes home to 3 to 5 parents a week describing what their child did well. We worked with a group of teachers in some of the highest need schools in Escambia County, Florida. They applied the 3 to 5 approach and surveyed their parents at the end of each month asking, How satisfied are you with your child's learning in Ms. ____ class? On a five point scale, over 90% of parents rated this question a "4" or "5" with 70% rating it a "5."

> Dear Ms. Johns,
> Timmy overcame his struggle with learning his multiplication tables this week. He mastered all required problems. I know you are very proud of Timmy. He worked extra hard to achieve this task.
>
> Ms. Krutch

Reward students who consistently perform well or exhibit good behavior. Remember, what gets recognized gets repeated. So, if we recognize good performance and behavior that's what we get more of.

Second, very specifically describe how students can improve their performance. When doing so, use rich descriptions that clearly delineate performance areas that need improvement. Say things like, "Your paragraph needs some improvement with organization. Work on making better transitions from one paragraph to another. Think about how each paragraph connects and use language to show that connection." This rich description provides much more information for students to use than do statements like "good work," "needs improvement," or "C."

Third, focus on how well rather than how rapidly students accomplished the learning target. Some students work more slowly than others but may achieve at an acceptable level. Learning is not about how fast students complete a task. We are interested in how close students are to hitting the learning targets. It may take some students longer to hit the targets. They, too, need to be judged on the quality of their work using the same criteria as those who got there sooner.

Fourth, focus on quality rather than quantity of student work accomplished. If we give students a large quantity of work to keep them busy, we aren't focused on how well they are learning the target at hand. Students working fewer problems well with an understood purpose produce better student learning results than students completing loads of work with a goal of "getting it done." Students easily recognize when we assign them work to keep them busy, especially when they view the amount of homework assigned and number of classroom worksheets distributed as irrelevant to learning. Therefore, instead of assigning them all odd problems at the end of a math chapter, assign them three to five problems to bring to class the next day. Integrate a formative assessment strategy into the next day's lesson to re-introduce and refine the previous day's lesson and to gauge how well students accomplished the learning target. They are more likely to think reflectively and complete three to five problems than twenty-five or thirty.

Fifth, focus on providing feedback about the learning task, not personalizing it to a student. We write feedback that recognizes student performance or behavior to help them improve or let them know they hit the mark. Share information that speaks to the specifics about a performance rather than making a judgment about the value of any student. Don't say, "Jonathon, you must be struggling with the work assigned. Again, you are way off target. How many times do we have to go over the state capitals?" Instead, say, "Jonathon, I noticed that all capitals of the southern states were correctly identified. Let's work on another section of the country and get those correct. I am going to give you a set of northern states. See if you can get those correct, as well."

Sixth, provide opportunities for students to express that they understand the feedback and what they need to do to improve. A quality feedback process is as much about students reflecting on the information as it is about them receiving it. The most productive reflections come when students receive descriptive feedback that includes identifying what they have done well and where they can improve. Remember, as students receive descriptive feedback on clearly defined learning expectations, they begin to take ownership of their learning. They become self-regulated learners wanting information they can use to reflect on what they need to do to get closer to hitting the learning targets. Each step of the way they gain confidence to become better and better learners.

As teachers we constantly create ways to collect and analyze information to share with students. Feedback can be applied by the teacher, by student peers, or through self-assessments. I provide some examples that we could use in our classrooms or could be used to trigger other ideas. The feedback strategies in this chapter provide much more than data collected – they specifically create ways for students to receive descriptive feedback about their performance.

FEEDBACK STRATEGIES

Remember, our weekly plans include learning targets and very specific actions students will engage in to achieve the target. We need to know how they are doing as they practice. So, along the way we must collect information to get a "pulse check" of their learning. Feedback strategies used for the purpose of formatively assessing students help us check the learning pulses of our students. Enjoy a few samples.

"Act On It Now" Notes

Act On It Now notes are "sticky" notes that teachers could use to place on student work. Post an "Act On It Now" note on students' assignments to specifically let them know how well they did and what they need to do to improve. The notes should be descriptive yet focused on one or two very specific improvement areas.

To determine how students have reduced their learning gaps, we could ask them to turn in their old work with the sticky note attached and the revised work. We quickly see a cohesive package of the old work, the note to the student, and the new work with improvements. Consequently, we directly focus on the specific corrective action the student completed. Our assessment of their work becomes clear and focused.

Also, students may use an "Act On It Now" note as an instructional tool. Students become reflective learners as we ask them to complete an "Act On It Now" note about their own work. If coached well by teachers, students could complete a note to help their peers. All this is to say, using "Act On it Now" notes could easily become part of a procedure or routine in our classrooms to provide students with opportunities to self-reflect about their learning and to receive feedback from others. No matter the assessor, "Act on It Now" notes serve as a tool used to communicate student assessment information focused on one or two needed areas of improvement.

*ActOnIt*NOW™

To: *Louise*
Date: *October 24, 2009*
Assignment: *Timeline for Colonization*

What could be improved:
Include all events in the time period of the 13 colonies in America. Carefully label each entry.

What you did well:
Your timeline was well organized and visually appealing. Using different colors for each colony demonstrated your knowledge of each of the colonies and helped with organization.

©Janet K. Pilcher

Time Out Card

At any time when students feel lost, behind, or frustrated they complete a "Time Out" card and give it to the teacher at the end of the class period. As teachers, we create our own procedures for how students turn in "Time Out" cards. The card includes the student's name, date, assignment/task, and answers the following question: what is the major barrier keeping you from learning? We coach students to write descriptive information to give us what we need to help them. If we are receiving numerous "Time Out" cards, we realize students aren't getting it! Stop, regroup, and try again with students.

Time Out!

Name:

Date:

Assignment / Task:

What is the major barrier keeping you from learning?

©Janet K. Pilcher

Red, Green, Yellow

When I taught high school math, I used a red, green, yellow formative assessment strategy. Each student had a red, green and yellow card as part of their daily materials. When teaching a math concept, I asked students to work a sample problem like one I had taught them how to solve. Before providing the answer and working the problem on the board, I would ask them to raise one of the cards with green meaning "I got it," yellow saying "Maybe, but not sure," and red representing, "Not happening." A quick glance at the colors provided a gauge indicating how students were doing on the learning target. This information helped me know when to move on, re-teach, or pay close attention to the groups of students who were not quite catching on.

The main purpose of this formative assessment strategy is to provide a pulse check about how students are doing as instruction takes place. An added bonus - students realize when they are raising more red cards than desired. Open the door for those students to seek additional help.

A secondary, but beneficial purpose focuses on rewarding success. To give all students chances to experience success, use this approach for students to practice something that will get a lot of green cards raised. It's great to see students build their confidence and recognize their own achievements. Intentionally create winning situations to positively reinforce students' current achievement levels using the red, green and yellow strategy. It's important to celebrate student wins along the way.

Thumbs Up, Thumbs Down

For younger students, we can apply a quick pulse check by asking them to give us a "Thumbs Up" or a "Thumbs Down." Often we model something we want students to emulate. We use examples and non examples as we demonstrate the desired learning behavior. Students give a "Thumbs Up" for a correct approach and "Thumbs Down" when viewing a non-example. Also, "Thumbs Up" and "Thumbs Down" can be used to get a quick read on students' desire to move forward with learning. We teach a concept, ask students to give a "Thumbs Up" if they are ready for us to move on.

Stoplight Report

As a teacher you could create a class stoplight report. The stoplight report includes actions teachers and students are doing each day to achieve the learning targets. Items placed in the green category represent actions that have been achieved; items placed in the yellow category signify concepts students need to continue to practice; and items placed in the red category mean that the actions are on hold for now until more yellows move to green. Items in the red category need quite a bit of attention before moving to yellow.

The stoplight report serves as an information tool for students. They can use it to self-assess their progress on achieving the learning targets and climbing the learning ladder. If their progress is in line with the class stoplight report, they are on target. If they have more reds and yellows than what the report indicates, they need additional assistance to get on track. Here students could complete the "Time Out" card to submit to the teacher.

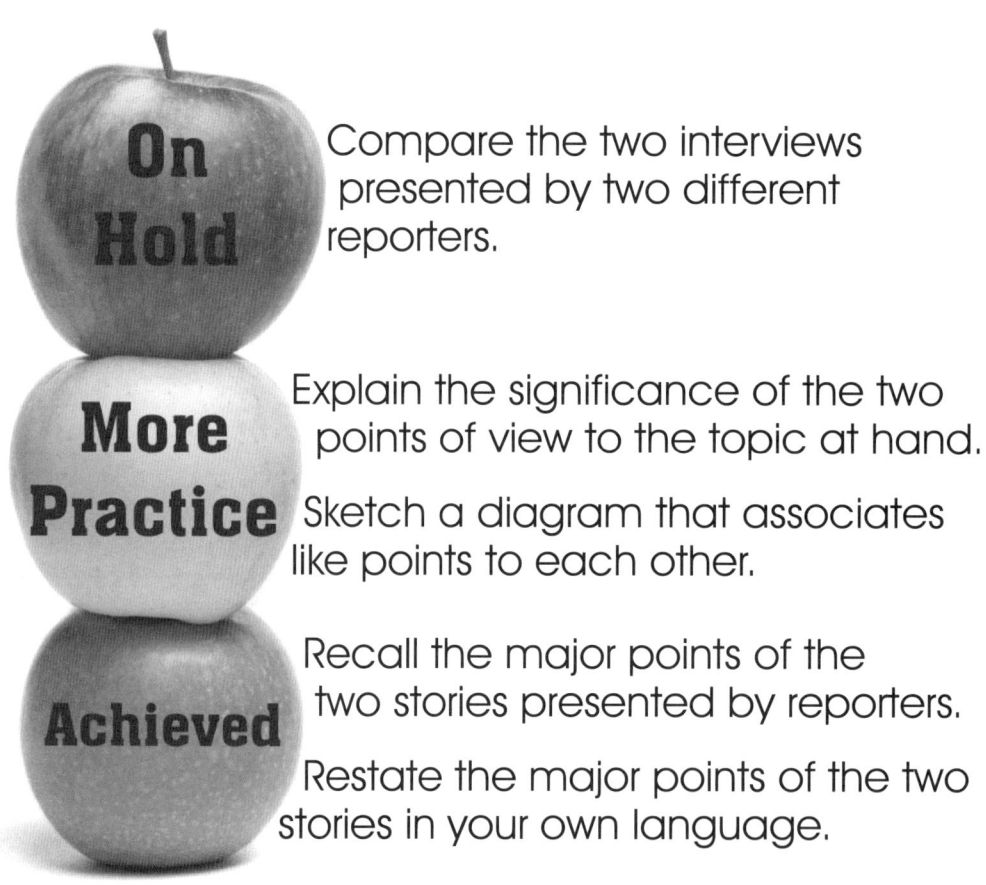

Student Rounding for Learning Outcomes[13]

One of the most successful practices healthcare professionals do with their patients is "rounding" on them. Think of a patient in a hospital. The doctor comes to the patient's room each day asking a very common set of questions. The doctor gathers formative information about the patient's well-being and establishes a relationship. When the doctor leaves the room, the patient feels cared about.

As teachers, we want to gather formative information about student learning, and we, too, want students to know we care about them and are concerned about their well-being. As often as we can, I suggest that teachers make rounds on their students. Let students know we will be rounding on them from time to time. Make sure students clearly understand the purpose of rounding – for students to know teachers are concerned about how well they learn. When a natural time arises, we ask students the following questions and take notes about what they say.

- What have you done well to hit the targets we are working on?
- What gaps are still occurring that are keeping you from hitting the targets?
- Do you have the information you need to hit the targets?

When using rounding as a formative assessment strategy we must be sincere about wanting to hear what students say. Remember our goal is to let students know we care and are concerned about them as individuals.

End of Class Survey

At the end of a class session, we could use a class survey to gather information from students about how well they believe they learned that day. Each student answers the question, similar to those in the survey below. We then analyze the responses and use the aggregate class information as an introduction to the next day's lesson. The surveys provide helpful information concerning where students believe they are in the learning process. Also, students like to see the information at the beginning of the next class. They compare their score to the class average to get a sense for how they compare to others. Being too far off the class average alerts them to pay close attention or to seek assistance.

End of Class Survey					
	Highly Agree	Agree	Neutral	Disagree	Highly Disagree
I learned something new today.	5	4	3	2	1
I valued what I learned today.	5	4	3	2	1
I feel like I mastered the learning target (s).	5	4	3	2	1
I have a good sense of where we are going next.	5	4	3	2	1
Learning gaps are keeping me from achieving the learning target (s).	5	4	3	2	1
What are the most important things you have learned today? What questions do you still have?					

Round Robin

Sometimes we want to engage our students as a group and get a learning pulse check. At the end of the day, we call for students to Round Robin. Students circle as a group. Each student has 15 seconds to debrief by answering the following two questions: what is working well and what areas still need work? If students agree with other students they snap their fingers three times.

Classroom Checkup

Although simple and less creative than some strategies, we hear from good teachers time and again how they constantly walk around the room with purpose. Specifically, we know that moving away from the front of the classroom or behind the desk automatically improves student engagement and gives us an opportunity to get a snapshot of how students are doing on the learning task at hand. We become engaged with them as they learn, sending a message that we care about them.

We suggest that teachers carry around a note pad as they walk around the room to record their observations. The Classroom Checkup is a note pad that includes date, period/ time, and class. The three rows on the pad read as follows: 1. class strengths, 2. class learning gaps, and 3. students needing attention.

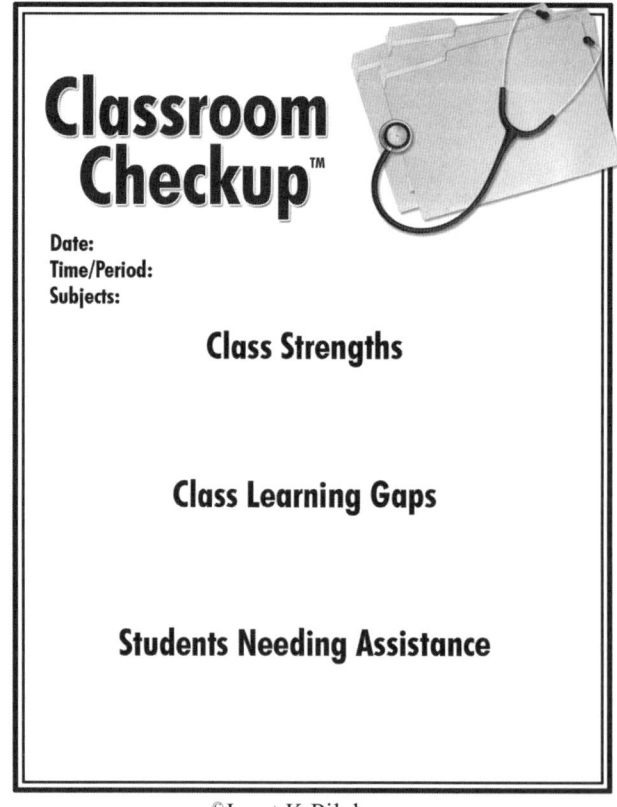

©Janet K. Pilcher

Light Locater (developed by a teacher Ms. Stacie Hammer)

After teaching a concept, distribute a Light Locater, which is a Stoplight with lines drawn by each color of the stoplight. Ask students to use the lines next to the red light to let the teacher know where students are really struggling. On the lines next to the yellow light, let the teacher know where things are just a little fuzzy. On the lines next to the green light, let the teacher know where students are good to GO!" The teacher collects each students' Light Locater, collates and analyzes the information, and uses the feedback to prepare for the next day's instruction

Show Me What You Know (developed by a teacher Ms. Stacie Hammer)

The teacher presents a question. Students have small white boards at their desk. They write the answer and the teacher says, "show me what you know." They show their white boards and she gets a pulse check indicating the number of students providing the correct answers and those still needing assistance.

Interactive Teaching

We can apply an interactive teaching approach in various ways. One important way is to model behavior highlighting the various aspects of learning steps we want students to demonstrate. Students watch us and reflect on what we are doing. We let them practice by emulating the learned behavior while receiving immediate feedback to help them know what they did well and where they need to improve. Take a look at Ms. Caddell's example. She put examples of word problems on the document camera and used bright markers to highlight questions, key phrases, and important numbers. Ms. Caddell applied this strategy to a whole group of students and then asked a student to come up and use the bright markers to help her complete the problem. So that everyone could practice, she gave students copies of the pages she used in whole class instruction. The students reviewed the pages as they used colored pencils to model this task on their own.

Buddy Systems

If students have a buddy to turn to when learning gets uncomfortable, they may feel less intimidated and more likely to take risks. A buddy answers questions, provides support, and enjoys learning with a partner. Buddies serve as peer coaches to each other – they focus on helping each other hit the learning targets. When we want quick feedback about where students are performing, we could say, Buddy Up!, indicating student buddies need to check-up on each other.

Minute Paper[14]

At the end of a class or instructional time, we could select several questions that help students reflect on their learning and provide us with good information about where students are in the learning process. Select two to three questions that students will answer in about a minute. Ask them to turn in the information to you or create a way for them to analyze each others' responses and report to the class. Sample questions might include:

- What was the most important (significant, crucial) thing you learned in today's class?
- What question(s) do you have about the material covered in today's class?
- What was the muddiest point in today's lecture?
- How can I help you learn the concept that is giving you the most trouble?
- List the key concepts from today's class.
- What question did I ask students today that helped you the most? The least?
- What examples did I use today that helped you the most? The least?
- What is the main application of the material we discussed today?

Some teachers tell us they like to gather more in-depth and reflective information from time to time using strategies such as journaling. Think about using these same questions or others like them when asking students to respond in a journal. Likewise, these questions could be used in mini-conferences with students.

Teach It

We hear people say – you learn something best when you teach it! Students learn what they know and don't know when we give them a concept to teach. Ask students to communicate the learning target, explain the concept, and provide an example. Classmates listen and complete a rating scale on how well they believe the concept presented is accurate with "5" representing the highest level of accuracy and "1" the lowest level. Share aggregate results using frequencies and mean ratings. This information can be used by students and the teacher as a discussion to reinforce learning a concept aligned to a learning target.

TEACH IT!					
Learning Target:					
Accuracy of Content:	5	4	3	2	1

Group Tests

I find that group tests work well for assessing where students stand on achieving a very specific learning target they need to know to move to the next target. Individually, students respond to a brief set of questions or problems tightly aligned to that one target. In groups of three to four, students compare their answers and determine the correct responses. Ask the groups how confident they are (green, yellow, red) about the correctness of their answers. All green cards indicate students are ready to move ahead. A majority of yellow cards says they are not as confident as they need to be. If we see red, back up and start again.

Rate My Work

Think about the process Amazon.com uses for individuals to rate their books or products. To provide a holistic evaluation of student work, students could ask other students to apply a "Rate My Work" scale to their work samples. Students shade in the smiley faces on the scale to determine work quality. The more smiley faces shaded by raters, the better the judgment of the work. A comments box is provided for students to describe their rating.

An average rating is calculated and the shading of the summary ratings is represented by full and partly shaded smiley faces. Therefore, students receive the average rating and the rating by each student with their comments attached.

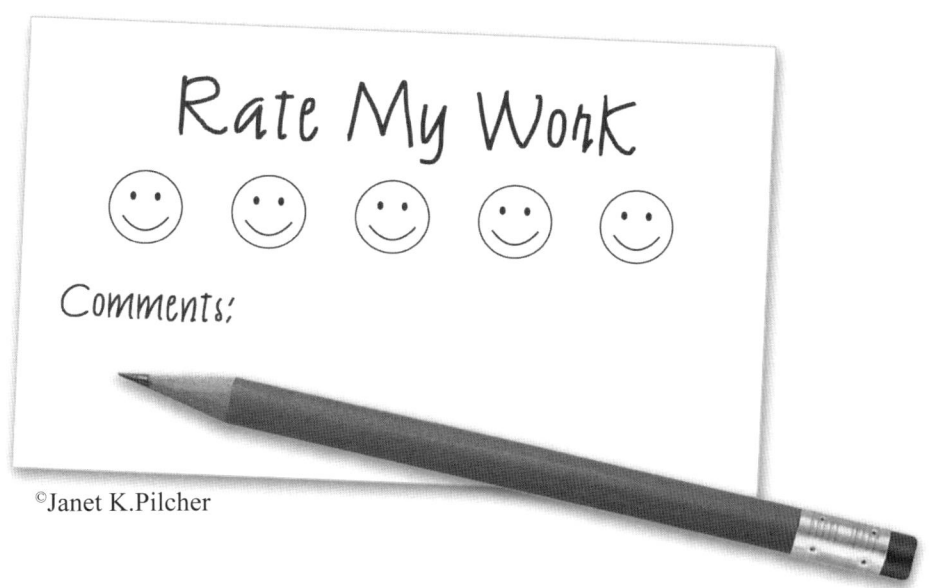

©Janet K.Pilcher

Wiki Trail

A Wiki allows users to freely create and edit Web page content. Let's say we give students a writing rubric that contains comprehensive information about content accuracy and good writing skills. They're to use this rubric to guide them to write a three paragraph essay. We assign either writing or editing roles to students. The writers begin by developing three paragraphs using a Wiki. A number of editors are assigned to each writer. The editors use the criteria with good descriptive information provided in the writing rubric to add to the content and make edits on the initial Wiki content. Each editor has an opportunity to enhance and improve the writing. When each Wiki is complete by each group, students read the other Wikis and use the rubric to evaluate the final products. For various writing assignments, we can change the roles students play making sure each student receives practice being the writer.

This formative assessment strategy completed by students to assess their own work and the work of others gives them opportunities to practice and reflect on their writing skills. In addition, the strategy presents a team effort that may help weaker writers feel less intimidated and gives strong writers an opportunity to further deepen their writing abilities. In addition, students do not have to be in class together at the same time to complete the assignment. The work is done on the web. A final bonus - students seem to find this instructional assessment activity helpful and fun.

Meeting of the Minds

Using examples and non examples of strong and weak work provide students with ways to identify their learning gaps and to improve their skills. Students hold a "Meeting of the Minds" to review and assess examples and non-examples of work we give them. Here we do not use the work of other students in their class. We want students to review the data of work samples, not evaluate the quality of work by other students.

Using assessment criteria and parameters we provide, students work with peers in a "Meeting of the Minds" group to discuss the work samples. The assigned group leader facilitates the discussion using a plus and minus chart. Students list the positive aspects under the plus section and the areas that need improvement under the minus section. Each group discusses the pluses and minuses of each work sample. The group then uses the plus/minus data for each work sample to place them in high, middle, or low performance categories. Leaders try to get group consensus to come to a "Meeting of the Minds." They are responsible for presenting the overall ratings of the samples and using the plus/minus data to explain why the groups made their decisions.

Student-Developed Assessment Tools

One important way for students to learn how to recognize quality work is to afford them opportunities to develop sample assessments, including scored response tests and performance assessments. To do this well, students need to know how to apply good test and performance assessment development criteria to create accurate and quality tools. Therefore, prior to asking students to develop assessments, we must teach them how to do this well. All types of benefits result from teaching students how to develop good assessment tools, including helping students become better test takers and reinforcing the deepest understanding of expectations.

To develop test items, students use the list of learning targets and create items they believe align to that target. They quickly see that to do this, they need to know the concept very well.

One way to involve students in the development of performance assessments or rubrics is to give them weak and strong work samples and ask them to brainstorm what makes the samples weak and strong. Students make a list and determine the types of things that are alike on the list. They collate the like items and then name what they think the items represent. Using the terms, the students create sentence descriptions revealing high, middle, and low performance. After exerting this much energy and thought, students internalize the criteria representing high quality work.

SUMMARY

The feedback strategies presented in this chapter represent one important part of the *Student Engagement Framework*. The process ties to Sadler's formative assessment theory presented two decades ago and reinforced a decade later by Black and Wiliam's meta-analysis results. In addition, my colleagues and I work with teachers every day and witness their students becoming more engaged learners who are achieving at improved levels. The formative assessment strategies are instructional in nature – they provide data to help teachers and students know where students are and where they need to improve. As important, many of the strategies offer students opportunities to reflect on their own work. I've found that when feedback strategies are applied, teachers and students alike become more engaged in daily learning and with each other. Teachers naturally leave their classrooms each day asking how well their students learned. Consequently, students know teachers care that they've learned. Use the feedback strategies in this chapter or create your own.

CHAPTER 7
—————— SUMMATIVE ASSESSMENT TOOLS ——————

Each day, students practice learning while being coached by their teachers and peers who provide feedback on small chunks of instruction. They receive pulse check assessments telling them what they are doing well, where they need to improve, and how to do so. They are then ready for teachers to judge them on how well they have accomplished the learning targets to achieve an overall learning goal.

Remember, only data from summative measures are averaged as part of a student's final grade. Within a 30 day time period, we plan segments of instruction that include scaffolds of learning targets. We create tools to use for summative purposes at the end of each instructional segment. So, within a month we may have around three to five summative measures recorded in our gradebook. This, of course, occurs after students practice the skills we intend to measure.

As we design summative assessment tools let's keep a particular frame of mind. We want students who know the answer to choose the correct response and for those who don't to respond incorrectly. Therefore, developing tests that achieve this goal means that we have developed a good test. We can create a classroom that engages students to learn and provides invaluable instruction. But if our summative assessment tool is not created in a way that measures what we want to measure and measures that well, student achievement fails to represent "true" achievement levels. Who loses? - our students. If a doctor does a thorough review of our illness but prescribes the wrong medical tests, our illness has a good chance of being misdiagnosed. What's at stake? – our lives. In our classrooms, wrong measures provide students and their parents with wrong information about their student achievement levels. Well designed measurement tools aligned to instruction could save our students' academic lives. This is serious business for us and our students.

We discussed in the previous chapters that our goal is to develop learning targets with aligned learning tasks that scaffold student learning. To do so, students must move through segments of instruction that begin with lower complexity levels of learning to those applications that require more complex skills.

What do we mean by complexity levels? Skills with lower complexity levels require students to recall or describe information as we discussed in Bloom's Taxonomy in Chapter 4. Students apply what is learned within the context in which the learning occurs. Students, who perform higher complexity skills, explain, analyze or synthesize information. They must apply the information learned in a different context from which it was learned.

As teachers we find ourselves moving in and out of complexity levels with students as we provide specific feedback to help them achieve the targets. Learning one target helps students learn the next and so on and once they apply the target at the most complex level, the learning targets aligned to lower complexity skills become easier for students. To judge student achievement levels, assessing both lower and higher level skills is important. We don't want to teach or assess one level at the expense of the other. We expect our students to achieve more complex skills. To do so, we must teach and evaluate their ability to achieve appropriate and aligned foundational skills to the learning task at hand. Just as learning targets scaffold instruction, summative assessments must evaluate the major blocks or segments of instruction along the way.

TEST BLUE PRINT

For developing tests or selecting developed tests, I recommend teachers use a simple test blueprint that includes the learning targets, number of questions for each target, and number of points assigned to each question. Teachers should share this blueprint with students at the beginning of the unit of instruction. This guides them on what they are expected to learn and how they will be judged once they have had time to practice learning tasks. Tests provide a mechanism to evaluate students' knowledge and their applications of that knowledge in a relatively quick way.

TEST BLUEPRINT		
Learning Target	**# of items**	**Points per item**

When creating a test blue print we want to develop a fair test that provides students with the best opportunity to show evidence that they have mastered the learning targets. Therefore, we must simultaneously consider three important things:

- The weight per item
- The complexity level of the learning target
- The amount of time students have to take the test

We don't want any item or types of items to be weighted too high. We want to have enough items on the test with appropriate points per item so that missing one or two items does not produce misinformation about "true" understanding of information learned. The complexity level of the learning targets will determine the complexity level of the test. Therefore, we don't want the test to be too easy or too difficult. Also, we need to consider the amount of time students have to take a test. Here is the rule of thumb when thinking about time needed for students to answer test questions.

Type of Question	Time Per Question
True-False	15-30 seconds
Multiple Choice (recall level)	30-60 seconds
Multiple Choice (higher complexity level)	60-90 seconds
Matching (5 premises, 6 responses)	2-4 minutes
Fill-in-the-blank (one word)	30 to 60 seconds

A teacher learning about developing test blueprints told us a story about her son. She took the sample copy of a test blueprint home to her son who was a sophomore in high school. She asked him if his teachers provided him with this type of information in his classes would he find it useful. She said he gave her a glazed look and said, of course. He told her that he would be clear about what he was expected to learn and it would help him study for his tests. Bingo! This is what we want for all of our students.

GUIDELINES FOR DEVELOPING TESTS

The goal when writing tests is to write items so that students who know the answer select the correct choice and those who don't select a wrong answer. Although this is difficult to do in an exact way, we should make this our goal as we develop tests. The guidelines presented in this section help us do just that.

All items need to follow two major guidelines. First, all items should align to specifically defined learning targets. Second, items should be written at a level below the students' reading ability. Unless testing reading, we don't want students to select the wrong answer because they are unable to read the question. With this in mind, let's turn to review specific guidelines for several popular types of questions.

Multiple Choice

A multiple choice item consists of a stem (the question), a series of options representing possible answers, one correct answer and distractors or options that are incorrect answers. The guidelines provided in this section can be used to develop test items or to evaluate items already developed by others. To explain the guidelines I provide a learning target and then an example and a non example sample question.

1. The stem clearly presents a problem or states a question and is stated without using extraneous information.

Learning Target: Given a sentence, identify the word that represents the verb of the sentence.	
Non Example	**Example**
Farmers grow many different types of crops on their farms. Sentences below represent the types of crops farmers grow and have underlined words. Choose the sentence where a verb is underlined. A. <u>Corn</u> grows in summer months. B. Farmers <u>pick</u> greens in the winter months. C. Farmers use <u>tractors</u> to plant gardens. D. Oranges are picked <u>from</u> trees.	Which sentence below has a correctly underlined verb? A. <u>Corn</u> grows in summer months. B. Farmers <u>pick</u> greens in the winter months. C. Farmers use <u>tractors</u> to plant gardens. D. Oranges are picked <u>from</u> trees.

2. Options are parallel in the type of content presented.

Learning Target: Describe characteristics/events that occur in the fall.	
Non Example	**Example**
Fall is the time of year A. Before summer B. Green leaves C. Halloween falls on October 31 D. When trees have no leaves	Which statement below represents something that is typical of the fall season? A. Green leaves change to orange and yellow. B. Heavy snow is forecasted. C. March winds blow. D. The highest temperature of the year occurs.

3. The grammar in the option should be consistent with the stem.

Learning Target: Identify a type of bird.	
Non Example	**Example**
An _____ is a type of bird. A. Cow B. Dog C. Donkey D. Eagle	The word below that represents a type of bird is a/an A. Cow B. Dog C. Donkey D. Eagle

4. Options avoid repetitive words.

Learning Target: State the reason baseball players practice hitting the baseball.	
Non Example	**Example**

Baseball players
 	
  A. Practice hitting the ball to get one base.
  B. Practice hitting a fly ball at every bat.
  C. Practice hitting the ball swinging hard.
	What do baseball players want to accomplish when they practice hitting the ball?
	
	  A. Get on base.
	  B. Hit a fly ball at every bat.
	  C. Swing as hard as they can.

5. Each distractor should be plausible. Stay away from writing distractors that contain humor or that are obviously wrong answers.

Learning Target: Determine the action that represents a classroom procedure.	
Non Example	**Example**

Where should you turn in your completed work at the end of class?
 	
  A. Kick it like a football.
  B. Pass the work to the front of the row.
  C. Place the work on the right corner of your desk.
  D. Raise your hand and give the work to the teacher.
	Where should you turn in your completed work at the end of class?
	
	  A. Hand the work to the person sitting on your right hand side.
	  B. Pass the work to the front of the row.
	  C. Place the work on the right corner of your desk.
	  D. Raise your hand and give the work to the teacher.

6. Words such as "except" and "not" that reverse meaning or words that accentuate meaning (least, most) of the stem or option should be underlined or placed in bold print if used. Stay away from using double negatives as represented in the item below. To make it a good question, the word "not" in the stem should be bold or underlined and no options should have the negative word, "not." The item below represents a poorly written item (no underline under not and a double negative)

Which item is not representative of a primary color?

A. Blue
B. Red
C. Not Blue
D. Yellow

7. Exclude options such as "all of the above" or "none of the above." Don't use them as a way to add additional options. It is best to choose three plausible options rather than four options that include adding all or none of the above because it seems too difficult to write a fourth plausible distrator.

8. Unless an order is more logical, place options in alphabetical order. This keeps students from thinking that you have created a sequence and pattern for choosing the right answer with specific lettered options. Tell students that you are developing the test with this approach so that they will not spend time trying to guess a pattern of responses you created as you developed the test. For example, if they have selected three letter A's in a row you don't want them to change an answer because they think they've selected too many A's.

You may notice from the good examples the stem poses a question. In many instances items are easier to write when you simply pose a question and then provide several response options.

Matching

Matching items are a special case of multiple choice items. More than one item has a representative set of options.

1. The options should be parallel in the content presented such as numbers or words representing a common subset of information. For example, a list of Presidents of the United States, a list of cities to represent state capitals, and a list of dates when events occurred. Don't mix and match cities, people, numbers, etc. as part of the choice options.

2. Items should include at least one more option than the number of questions to reduce guessing. However, too many options if not meaningful reduce the quality of the matching items.

True False

True-False items are some of the most difficult to write because the answer has to be completely true or completely false. It takes some thought to make sure your item aligns to this guideline as well as others provided below.

1. The item is unequivocally true or false.

2. The item represents a single proposition and is not joined by the word "and."

3. An incorrect item is plausible.

4. The item excludes extraneous information.

5. Words such as "except" and "not" that reverse meaning or words that accentuate meaning (least, most) of the stem or option should be underlined or placed in bold print if used.

6. Adjectives and adverbs that imply indefinite time occurrences or absolute meanings should be excluded from the item, such as never, often, sometimes, and always.

Fill-in-the-Blank

Sometimes we want students to recall some information by placing a word in a sentence where we leave space with a blank. To write good fill-in-the blank items consider all the guidelines presented.

1. A single or homogeneous set of responses represent the correct response.

2. The blank represents a key word.

3. Blanks are placed at the end of the item.

Learning Target: Select a primary color.	
Non Example	**Example**
_____ is a primary color. (blank in front)	One primary color is _____.
One primary _____ is blue. (not a keyword)	Blue is called a _____ color.

4. The number of blanks should be limited so that they do not interfere with the content of the stem.

5. The length of the blank (line where the answer goes) should be the same length for each question. Longer words do not need longer blanks. All blanks should be the same size.

6. A sentence from a book should not be copied to represent a fill-in-the blank item.

Keep these guidelines handy as you design your classroom tests or analyze tests included in your textbooks or developed by other teachers. Please keep in mind that test items must align to the learning targets you teach. Before evaluating the quality of an item, first ask does this item align to the learning targets listed in the test blueprint. Also, consider a few additional tips as you design and administer the test to students.

- Write clear directions;
- Let students know the number of points per item;
- Place all like items together;
- Read the directions and ask students if anything is unclear;
- Answer their questions to clarify directions, not coach them on how to answer;
- Encourage them to do well;
- Answer time consuming questions last; and
- Encourage them to mark items for later review and changing of answers.

We judge our success by how well students learn. Summative assessment data provide the verdict for us to judge the success of our students and therefore, our success. Let's do everything we can to support students by writing good test items.

GUIDELINES FOR WRITING PERFORMANCE ASSESSMENT TOOLS ───────

Sometimes we want to evaluate a student's product or performance. Here, teachers design performance assessment tools - what many people refer to as rubrics. Students complete a performance task while using a rubric as a learning guide. A quality rubric includes performance criteria and/or narratives and a measurable scale specifically defining achievement expectations. This tool should be provided to students at the beginning of the instructional unit.

I advocate that better performance assessment tools have very specific performance criteria and a narrative description of, at minimum, the accomplished level of a task. The scale attached to the narrative can be dichotomous (meets or does not meet), scaled with less descriptive narrative for each scale level (three or more levels), or scaled and descriptive for each level presented. The Six Trait Writing Assessment developed by the Northwest Regional Laboratory is an example of a highly descriptive performance assessment tool[15].

Before considering the scale to use, a good performance assessment tool must have the first four components below, three of which we discussed in previous chapters.

- A final learning target
- Scaffolds of aligned learning targets
- A performance or learning task
- Performance criteria
- Narrative descriptions using the performance criteria

I provide two examples at the end of this chapter, one focused on students creating a concept map to demonstrate their abilities to relate one thing to another and the second one focused on students developing a well organized paragraph. The process for creating a performance assessment using the paragraph example includes scaffolds of learning targets, descriptors used to assess the quality of an organized paragraph, and narrative language aligned to the descriptors.

Let's take a closer look at designing performance assessments using the relationship example, a concept map. The 30 day learning target and the scaffolding of targets reinforces what we have learned thus far. For each learning target students practice learning tasks and receive coaching and feedback each step along the way. The scaffolds represent the visible acts students take as they climb the learning ladder. Students will produce a product or demonstrate their performance on a very well defined learning task used to assess their achievement. For this example, students are asked to create a concept map to show relationships of words and in this case, words that relate to living things.

Be careful not to make a common mistake. I've heard teachers identify the assessment tool as the product – the concept map in this example. The concept map is simply a way to collect learning data. The concept map alone does not serve as an assessment. Rather we have to apply an assessment tool to judge the correctness of the skill being evaluated - students being able to show their ability to relate words to each other.

We apply this skill to students' understanding of science content focused on living things. So students are learning content and how to relate words to each other. For students to do well on this learning task they have to grasp the content knowledge. That is, they need to know the definition of living things and examples of things that have life. In this particular, example living things include those things that represent animals and plants. Also, students need to be able to know what it means to relate one thing to another. Knowing about plants and animals combined with how to explain how the characteristics of plants and animals relate to each other help students develop an accurate concept map.

The performance criteria are descriptors that represent the student's ability to apply the skill. We could choose to use the descriptors or take one more step and write a narrative description that explains the desired performance. From there, we create scales of measures ranging from high to low performance. Many scales contain five levels of measures that are easily transferable to our common letter grading system.

Developing performance assessments is time consuming, but once developed we can apply the same tool when assessing the same skill set. For example, no matter the content area we can use the same performance assessment tool with the skill set associated with relating words and using a concept map as a way for students to demonstrate their performance. The concept map allows us to assess our students' abilities to achieve the skill on how to relate words and thoughts to each other. If students are able to achieve the relationship skills, then we have confidence they have mastered the content skills.

When using the performance assessment criteria for formative rather than summative assessment purposes we provide specific feedback to students on each aspect of the criteria so that they know what they do well and where they need to improve. In this instance, the tool is used to coach students as they are learning. They know what they can do well and where their gaps are so that they can spend time practicing skill identified.

SUMMARY

The averaging of numbers on summative assessment tools is included in a student's end-of-term grade. The stakes are high – the grades determine if students pass or fail, move to the next grade level, have to repeat courses, or gain acceptance to a certain college. With this in mind, we should pay close attention to the quality of our summative assessment tools and the way we administer them to students. We've discussed that applying good alignment practices supported by the *Student Engagement Framework* motivates students to engage in learning and to achieve at their highest potential. Our classrooms focus less on teaching to tests and more on aligning and integrating learning targets, learning tasks, feedback strategies and summative assessment tools. This does not mean classroom and standardized tests are unimportant. The pressure reduces for teachers and students because students are learning each day they walk into their classrooms - not for the sake of scoring a particular score but for the sake of learning.

• • • • • • • • • • • • • 30 Day Learning Target • • • • • • • • • • • • • •
Given a set of words, create a picture to show the relationship of the words.

Scaffolds of Learning Targets
- Define living things.
- Identify words associated with living things.
- Define the words associated with living things.

- Given a set of words, determine if the word is associated with living things.
- Sort words into those that represent living things and those that do not.
- Given words associated with living things, describe how one word connects to another.
- Develop a sentence to show how one word connects to another.

- Given a set of words associated with living things, select the combination of words that connect to each other.
- Explain how each word connects to others.
- Develop a sentence to show how each word connects to another.

- Given a completed concept map analyze the connections that are correct and incorrect.
- **Given a set of words, produce a concept map on living things to show the relationship of the words.**
  [Note: The product should look like the diagram below]

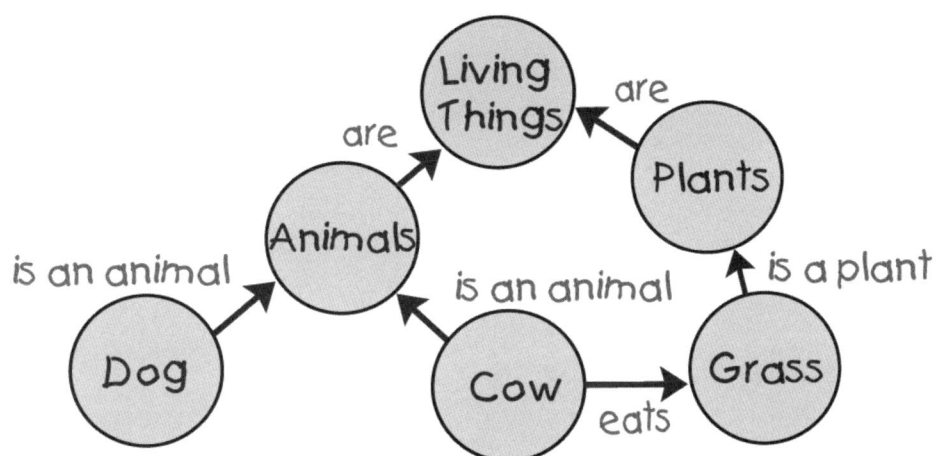

**Sample provided on website (Educational Technology Center, Wheeling Jesuit University, 2004)

Performance Criteria
- Words on the concept map relate to each other.
- Arrows that connect the words are in the correct direction.
- Arrows that connect the words represent correct relationships and no relationships are missed.
- The relationship of the terms is accurate and adds to the reader's knowledge of how the words are related to each other.

Narrative Description
The organization of the concept map clearly shows the reader key terms that relate to living things. The structure of the concept map, along with the direction of the arrows, clearly shows the reader how the terms are related to one another. As the readers read the words on the arrows that connect the terms, they are able to get a clear picture of how the terms relate and their relationship to one another.

Given three prompts, select one of the prompts and write a well organized paragraph that responds to the prompt.

Scaffolds of Learning Targets
- Define the characteristics of a paragraph that is well organized.
- Given a paragraph with underlined sentences, classify the underlined segments as good or bad organization.
- Given several paragraphs, choose the weak and strong examples of a well organized paragraph.
- Use the performance criteria to analyze the quality of a given paragraph.
- Given an unorganized paragraph, assemble the paragraph into an organized one.
- Develop a well-organized paragraph.

Performance Criteria
- An introduction, middle and end are easy to see.
- Sequencing makes sense and helps the reader comprehend the passage.
- Details seem to fit where they are placed.
- Thoughtful transitions clearly show how ideas connect.

Narrative Description
The organization of the writing lets readers easily recognize the central idea of the passage. The order and structure of the writing makes the passage easy to follow and understand. Any details included in the paragraph enhance the meaning of the passage. As readers read the passage the transitions help them move easily from one thought to another.

CHAPTER 8
30 DAY AND WEEKLY PLANS

As you have seen, creating and communicating learning targets are important first steps we use to effectively engage students to learn. The scaffolding of learning targets and the learning tasks we create help us collect student learning data. As students practice those tasks they receive feedback on what they did well and where they need to improve.

Bottom line – we want students to own their learning. When students know what is expected of them and receive feedback along the way, they become owners rather than renters of their learning. They enter our classrooms each day focused on the learning targets and ready to work with the teacher and other classmates to accomplish the tasks at hand. Learning becomes purposeful, and results become achievable.

As students work each day to achieve the learning targets, we keep the learning momentum going for students by recognizing good performance and encouraging them to improve. We coach students and provide them with ways to coach each other. Students come to class every day feeling hopeful and optimistic they will climb to the top of the learning ladder – they are eager to engage with others to learn.

Teachers guided by the *Student Engagement Framework* put learning in motion as students climb the learning ladder faster and faster and higher and higher. As students experience success their momentum begins to build. They become more engaged and feel better about themselves.

Let me introduce you to Ms. Atkins. She teaches 9th and 10th graders in an alternative education school. Students who are in trouble with the law or who have been suspended from school join her in class. This is what Ms. Atkins wrote after applying the 30 Day Plan for the first time.

When I sat in class and listened to the 30 day plan I was thinking to myself, 'okay, I'll give this a try but I'm not really sure how this is going to work with my students. The overriding issue with students in a dropout prevention program is VOP (violation of probation). Students can be sailing along at a decent clip and then, boom! Violation of probation occurs and they're out of class until they meet with the judge, then they're back in class, then they've got court so that is another missed day. It is a revolving door of attendance, at times.

I wanted to design my lessons to enable students to pick up easily if they missed a day or a week. Basically, I was stumped as to how to accomplish this in a 30 day time period. Many of my classes are designed to enable students to work at their own pace. It is as if I have differentiated lesson plans for each student because I may have a student in 9th grade English who just needs one credit of English and one credit of Math then he or she is ready to graduate and I may have another student who is taking English for the first time after being out of school for three years. This same student may need sixteen other credits before he or she will be eligible for graduation.

I aligned my learning target with a state benchmark which students are expected to demonstrate proficiency on the state test and a benchmark in which students need to master in order to write effectively. Then I was stumped again as to how to align my daily lesson plans with the learning target and still allow for students to float in and out of the classroom if VOP occurs. It would be impossible to do an hour and fifteen minute lesson each day that builds on the lesson from the day before. Each lesson had to align with my learning target and be an independent lesson or one with very little carry over from the day before. Independent lessons would allow for a student just returning to join right in to the class activity. If a student returned but felt that he or she couldn't do the work due to an absence caused by a stay in a juvenile center then disruption would ensue. I decided to use twenty minute lessons and activities which would allow plenty of time for review.

Every day I started with a quick review of the day before. (I mean, very quick.) After the review, I went right into the lesson and then the activity for practice. After the practice activity, I would collect the students' papers and then on the very first day, I did something I don't normally do—I went over the answers immediately. Now, I had the students' papers but since I had just collected them, they were fairly current on the answers they had written down. To my utter surprise, they were very interactive with me on the responses. So, the next day, I did the same thing; I collected the papers and

72

went over the answers. This routine went on for several days. About the 6th or 7th day, my principal walked in with a representative to show me a Mimio board. After I collected the papers, I stopped class for twenty minutes and we watched the Mimio presentation. The representative left and my students just sat there staring at me. One boy in the back said, "She's gone now, will you go over the answers so we know how we did?" I was so delighted to learn that my students had been sitting there waiting for "normal class" to resume. We started right back into discussing the answers.

Each day I noticed my students gained more and more confidence with their answers. It was work but I had all of their papers marked for them by the next day when they arrived. I wrote comments on their papers as to why a sentence would or would not work instead of using a check or an "x". After week one, students were entering class and asking, "What are we doing today, Mrs. Atkins?" and "Should we get into pairs, today?" I loved that they were so in tune to the class and I loved having the class run so smoothly.

I had some students enter after returning from a drug rehab program or a VOP incident and I barely had a chance to talk with them. My current students knew the ropes so well that they instructed the returning students as to where to sit for pairing and furthermore, told the returning students there would be a review followed by a lesson and they would be able to work with a buddy and instructed them to "not worry" about being absent. It was amazing! I had dropout prevention students assisting with lesson plans involving conventions for writing.

The change I made along the way was allowing my students to work in pairs more often. Initially, I had planned only 3 or 4 activities to be completed in pairs. However, my students appeared to glean more from peer feedback. Interestingly, because of attendance issues, my students did not end up working with the same partner every day so they were exposed to different ideas and assistance on a daily basis. I think the variety helped each student.

The other change I made immediately was allowing for discussion and feedback immediately, which fulfilled the immediate gratification side of teenagers. The discussions were a help to me just as much as they were a help to my students. I was able to form assessments from the discussions regarding comprehension and make adjustments for the next day's lesson accordingly. Additionally, I had each student's paper from that day's activity to check comprehension and progress.

I didn't grade all the work my students completed but I read all of it to check for comprehension and progress. I wrote comments on everything *they turned in. This is the first time they didn't ask, "Is this going to be graded?" I have some students who will not work if I don't grade something but with this plan, they were working for comments. It made me realize how important it is for me to keep feedback personalized for my students—it's not the grade, it is the assessment—they want to know how well they did, how can they improve, what exactly did I like about their sentences, what would work a little better, what made me laugh, what sounds like poetry, etc. A grade is just a letter or numbers at the top of their paper.*

However, parents and the school board members like to see grades so I gave my students a summative assessment at the end of each week. I produced the assessments. The first two were assessments students worked on individually, the third one they worked on as a pair and the fourth was, again an individual effort. My students made A's and B's on their assessments. Every student in the class (every one of them) could identify and distinguish between the implied and stated main idea in a paragraph.

I don't see me ever abandoning the 30 day plan. It was a huge success in my classroom. My students responded so positively. I was in awe at how they remained engaged. I am overwhelmed at the progress as indicated on my students' assessments. I would never have thought to try this; I never would have thought this to work with my classroom but it was a great success. Aside from the obvious of having a target to reach for every day, which kept me focused and able to keep the students on track, I wonder if the structure and routine of the 30 day plan is especially beneficial to dropout prevention students because it offers some structure and stability that many are missing in other areas of their lives. I noticed that they really enjoyed having the constant daily formative assessments in the form of discussions and they couldn't wait to get their papers back as soon as they walked in to class the next day. I would have never guessed that this demographic group would respond so positively to the 30 day plan. I feel like I've discovered a secret to help my students build upon their skills, build up their confidence, and allow them time to practice and produce.

Similar to Ms. Aktins' suggestion and the Black and Wiliam research findings, I've discovered struggling students benefit the most from teachers applying the *Student Engagement Framework*. However, all students benefit because they perform better when given specific feedback and when they are recognized for good work.

30 DAY PLANNING APPROACH

So, how do the strategies presented in previous chapters become manageable? To assist teachers I created a 30 day and weekly planning process for teachers to use. Why? As teachers, we know that if we lose students in a 30 day period, they likely will remain lost an entire semester and even a school year. Also, we can wrap our minds around what we and our students can accomplish in 30 days. We can clearly communicate and describe what learning looks like for students. Moving too far beyond 30 days becomes difficult to explain and is less specific and focused for students.

As you can see in the SEF diagram the 30 day plan and the weekly plans encompass the components of the *Student Engagement Framework* that leads to student learning results. Don't get hung up on the number '30.' Thirty days for some teachers means every month, actually 20 school days. Thirty days for other teachers means 30 actual teaching days. A 30 Day Plan usually falls somewhere between 20 and 30 actual teaching days and fluctuates for each 30 day time period. The total number of school days connected to the 30 Day Plan will depend on the overall learning targets and the scaffolds of those targets into small segments of instruction.

Over a 30 day time period summative assessments normally occur for each segment of instruction or about every 4 to 6 days, let's say. We also recommend that students achieve at an expected level on a cumulative 30 day assessment. This assessment allows us to triangulate or cross check students on how well they achieved the learning targets. For example, a student may not have performed well on the first summative assessment aligned to the first segment of targets, but after more practice over the 30 day period, this student achieved at a higher level on the same set of learning targets. We recommend that this highest level is more representative of the student's performance. To learn more about how this is accomplished, refer to a book written by me and my colleague, Dr. Robin Largue, *How to Lead Teachers to Become Great: It's All About Student Results.*[11]

30 DAY PLANS

Let's focus on completing 30 Day Plans to see how scaffolds of learning targets and tasks take shape and feedback strategies align to them. Figure 8.1 displays the first step of the 30 Day Plan. Before instruction begins, we work individually or with a team to complete the components. First, we define the final or 30 day learning target(s) students will be expected to perform. These targets are usually created beyond the knowledge level on Bloom's taxonomy chart. Then we create weekly targets and determine summative assessment tools we will use to assess an instructional segment of targets. Teachers can use the 30 Day Plan in Figure 8.1 to record the information just described. The 30 Day Plan then serves as the guide we use to design daily learning targets, learning tasks, and feedback strategies.

30 DAY PLAN		

Date for Plan Implementation:
State Standard:
30 Day Learning Target(s):
30 Day Summative Assessment Tools:

	Week One	
Weekly Learning Targets		
Summative Assessments		
	Week Two	
Weekly Learning Targets		
Summative Assessments		
	Week Three	
Weekly Learning Targets		
Summative Assessments		
	Week Four	
Weekly Learning Targets		
Summative Assessments		

Figure 8.1 30 Day Plan
©Janet K. Pilcher

A quick, yet important sidebar. All teachers confront the requirement of aligning their instruction to standards. The 30 day learning targets should only align to state standards teachers are "assessing" not just "covering." To show true alignment, we need to unpack every standard or deconstruct the language of standards to identify key skills within a given standard. To learn more, see *Aligning Instruction to Standards: Just Ask Andie* at *whosengaged.net.*[16]

The 30 Day Plan provides a guide for how we outline the weekly learning targets and the summative assessments of those targets. From this outline, we create aligned weekly plans.

Putting the 30 Day Plan into action, we turn to Ms. Caddell's plan on teaching word problems to her first grade students at Lipscomb Elementary School. Figure 8.2 displays her 30 Day Plan.

30 DAY PLAN: WORD PROBLEMS

30 Day Learning Targets: Solves the word problem using accurate calculations
30 Day Summative Assessment: Written Assessment

Week 1 March 9-13	
Weekly Learning Targets	<ul><li>Defines necessary and unnecessary information</li><li>Distinguishes between necessary and unnecessary information in the word problem</li><li>Identifies numerical values needed to solve the word problem</li><li>Identifies key question within the word problem</li><li>Identifies indicator words within the question (in all, how many more, how many are left, etc.)</li></ul>
Summative Assessments	Performance assessment: student identifies components of the word problem and explains the meaning of each component.
Week 2 March 16-20	
Weekly Learning Targets	<ul><li>Identifies key question within the word problem</li><li>Identifies indicator words within the question (in all, how many more, how many are left, etc.)</li><li>Distinguishes between key words that indicate subtraction and key words that indicate addition</li><li>Determines what operation is indicated by the key words</li></ul>
Summative Assessments	Written assessment: Given a set of word problems, student will circle the question in the word problem, underline the key words, and indicate if subtraction or addition should be used to solve.
Week 3 March 23-27	
Weekly Learning Targets	<ul><li>Sketches a picture that represents information presented in the word problem</li><li>Develops a math sentence that represents the information presented in the word problem.</li></ul>
Summative Assessments	Written assessment: Given a set of word problems, student will sketch a picture and/or write a math sentence that represents the information presented in the word problem.
Week 4 March 30- April 3	
Weekly Learning Targets	<ul><li>Represents information presented in a word problem with a math sentence and picture (if needed)</li><li>Solves word problem using subtraction accurately</li><li>Solves word problem using addition accurately</li></ul>
Summative Assessments	Written assessment: Given a set of word problems student will solve using accurate addition and subtraction methods.

Figure 8.2 Ms. Caddell's 30 Day Plan

Once again let's revisit the *Student Engagement Framework*. Teachers design 30 day and weekly plans and apply them with their students. As students are learning, they clearly understand the learning targets and how their learning tasks help them achieve the targets. Students and teachers alike provide continuous feedback as students practice. Once they have practiced enough, students complete an assessment activity where the teachers use the assessment information to judge their performance. The goal – for students to achieve the learning goals.

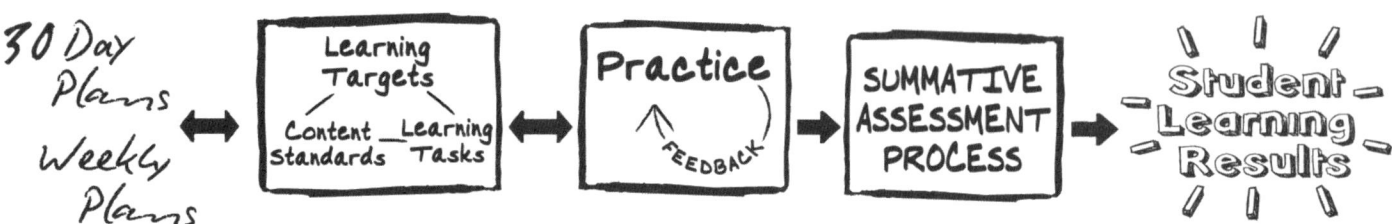

So, we have our 30 Day Plan. Now what? We move to complete weekly plans. To do so, we need to reflect on four questions:

- What will students need to know and be able to do to achieve the weekly learning targets? *(daily learning targets written in measurable terms)*
- What will I do this week to help students achieve the daily learning targets so that students can achieve the weekly learning targets? *(learning tasks)*
- How will I know if students achieve the daily learning targets so that students can achieve the weekly learning targets? *(feedback strategies –pulse check)*
- How will I communicate progress on the learning targets to students each day? *(feedback strategies - communication)*

We translate these reflections into action. We do this by using the 30 Day Plan to develop weekly plans. Some teachers tell us that creating a concept map or some sort of graphic organizer helps them determine what students need to know and do in week one, week two, week three and week four to achieve the 30 day learning targets. Keep in mind that using capability verbs from the learning taxonomy in Chapter 4 to design learning targets each week helps us scaffold students' learning.

Let's turn our attention back to Mr. Burt's lesson presented in Chapter 5 that included scaffolds of learning targets, aligned learning tasks, and applied feedback strategies. Mr. Burt completed a 30 Day Plan that guided him as he created his weekly plans. Take a close look at Mr. Burt's 30 Day Plan in Figure 8.3.

30 DAY PLAN: COMPOSITION OF VIEWPOINT

Date for Plan Implementation: February 15, 2010
State Standard: Analyze various points of view of text.
30 Day Learning Targets: Compose a news story presenting an opposite point of view from that given.
30 Day Summative Assessment Tools: Performance Assessment focusing on the skill sets aligned to the 30 day learning target

Week One	
Weekly Learning Targets	<ul><li>Recall the major points of two stories presented by two reporters.</li><li>Restate the major points of the two stories.</li><li>Explain the significance of the two points of view.</li><li>Sketch a diagram that associates like points to each other.</li><li>Compare the two news stories presented by two different reporters.</li></ul>
Summative Assessments	Paper and pencil tests of sample points of view and main idea. Part of preformance assessment for the given skill.
Week Two	
Weekly Learning Targets	<ul><li>Recall the major points of two stories presented by two news articles.</li><li>Restate the major points of the two stories.</li><li>Explain the significance of the two points of view.</li><li>Sketch a diagram that associates different viewpoints.</li><li>Contrast the two news stories presented by two different reporters.</li></ul>
Summative Assessments	Paper and pencil tests of sample points of view and main idea. Part of preformance assessment for the given skill.
Week Three	
Weekly Learning Targets	<ul><li>Identify main points of given information and data from two sources.</li><li>Explain the main points.</li><li>Sketch a diagram to compare and contrast information.</li><li>Compare and contrast information given to create a story.</li></ul>
Summative Assessments	Preformance assessment used for 30 day learning target.
Week Four	
Weekly Learning Targets	<ul><li>Identify main points of a given news story.</li><li>Explain the main points.</li><li>Generate points that oppose the viewpoint of the data source.</li><li>Sketch a diagram to contrast the opposing points to the news story.</li><li>Given a point of view, create a news story with the opposite viewpoint.</li></ul>
Summative Assessments	Cumulative paper and pencil test. Preformance assessment used for 30 day learning target.

Figure 8.3. Mr. Burt's 30 Day Plan

From Mr. Burt's 30 Day Plan he took each week's learning targets and wrote daily targets to scaffold instruction so that he could create aligned learning tasks and feedback strategies. Remember, daily tasks may represent more than one day. Daily refers to a logical chunk of instruction that needs to be taught for students to hit the final targets. The first thing Mr. Burt did was transfer the weekly learning targets from his 30 Day Plan to his four weekly plans. An example of this step for week one is provided in Figure 8.4.

WEEK ONE		
Weekly Learning Target:	**Compare two news stories presented by two different reporters.**	
Daily Learning Targets	**Learning Tasks**	**Feedback Strategies**
Recall the major points of the two stories presented by two reporters.		
Restate the major points of the two stories.		
Explain the significance of the two points of view.		
Sketch a diagram that associates like points to each other.		
Compare two news stories presented by two different reporters.		

Figure 8.4 Mr. Burt's Weekly Learning Targets in a Weekly Plan

Let's go one more step. On the next page look at Mr. Burt's learning tasks and feedback strategies for his **first** daily learning target for **week one.** (Figure 8.5)

If Mr. Burt has a 50 minute time block it most likely takes him two days to cover this daily goal. On the other hand, the daily target could be addressed with students in a one day, 90 minute time block. The way you actually schedule time allocated to daily learning targets and tasks depends on the time blocks of instructional time you have within a given day. Keeping this in mind you could add a "time column" to the chart to help you budget the time you plan to spend. Remember, the goal is for students to achieve each daily learning target so that they can achieve the weekly and then the 30 day learning targets. Therefore, time must be adjustable and flexible to ensure all students hit the targets.

When we follow a 30 Day Plan (Figure 8.3) and lay out our weekly plans using the charts in Figure 8.4 and 8.5, we connect the dots for students to help them learn. We also connect the dots for ourselves. I assert that many students fail because they cannot connect the dots as they attempt to learn. The *Student Engagement Framework* described in this book helps teachers do just that for students.

Weekly Learning Target:	Compare the two interviews presented by the two different reporters.	
Daily Learning Targets	**Learning Tasks**	**Feedback Strategies**
Recall the major points of the two stories presented by two reporters.	To refresh students' memory, provide about 5 to 7 minutes of instruction on main ideas and supporting details. Show the clip of the first reporter. Ask students to jot down what they believe to be the main points of the reporter's viewpoint. Ask students to get into their previously assigned groups of four, and assign a group leader for the day. In their groups, ask students to discuss what they believe to be the main points and to record those points on the post-it-note chart paper pad. Ask two group leaders to place their groups' sheets of paper on the recording wall. Then ask all groups to talk about how their items compare with the two groups' posted work. They have different color dots assigned to each group. After a 3 minute discussion, the group leader will place a dot on all items their group believes to be the main points using all group data on the wall. Post an empty sheet. If after reviewing the groups' information, a group believes a point has been missed by all groups, the group leader places that point on the empty sheet. Dots can also be placed on the points presented on that sheet. Provide a chart to students for them to complete.	Place the main points of the two reporters on the white board and ask students to check to see how well they did. If students missed main points altogether, provide that information to students and ask them to add it to their charts. Then enter into a discussion trying to close any gaps of students who missed the main points. If needed reintroduce the difference between main points and supporting details. Use the data in the charts to help make this point. Ask students to turn in their charts. On the top left hand corner ask them to write the word, green (meaning 'got it'), yellow (meaning 'getting there'), or red (meaning 'didn't get it').

Figure 8.5 Sample Learning Tasks and Feedback Strategies for Mr. Burt's
First Learning Target for Week 1

Whew! Undoubtedly this approach takes our time and good thinking. But, the outcomes for our students are priceless. Few students come into our classrooms naturally able to create the thinking process needed to work their way through class activities. Most students, especially those who struggle, can't build this type of cognitive framework on their own. They depend on their teachers to do this with them until they are able to transfer the process of learning to most any situation, even taking standardized tests. That is, they learn to transfer the ability to think, reason and process information because we have taught them how to do so. We can't afford to turn our backs on those who need us most. Let's view Ms. Jones in action and the results her students achieved. Ms. Jones teaches at-risk 3rd grade students.

This year I was commissioned to take on the task of teaching a group of last year's third graders who scored level one on the reading portion (the lowest possible level) of the state test. The make-up of this group of students is a wide and varied group. In this group of students, I have eighteen students; ten males and eight females. Four students have learning disabilities, three are language impaired, one is an English Language Learner, one is a diabetic whose blood sugar was low on the previous year's testing, two moved in from out of state, two are from another school in the district, two are homeless, one has a severe vision problem, and two were not motivated to do any kind of reading. One male student was retained in third grade. He scored lower on his state reading test the second time than he did the first time. Fourteen of these students are on free and reduced lunches and are from low-socioeconomic homes.

At the beginning of the year I realized after working with these students that most of them had given up on learning. They had poor self-esteem and did not feel as though they could learn. I knew that if they were going to make progress, I needed a miracle. I started to investigate ways to motivate this group. After the first testing results, I had ten in the red zone, low group, seven in the yellow zone, still below level, and one in the green zone, on grade level.

I decided to teach cause and effect since this is an important skill that is transferred across the curriculum to social studies and science. Also, previous test information indicated that these students were very confused on this concept. I knew I had to start at the low level of Bloom's Taxonomy and worked my way up to the higher order thinking skills. These students were missing so many basic skills. As I started to plan, I looked for ways to make learning fun and interesting. Once I started teaching cause and effect, I taught it every way I could. I taught cause and effect through read alouds and simple classroom happenings. The students began to really get involved in the learning.

Since I have a 90 minute reading block, I decided to devote 30 to 40 minutes each day teaching this skill. I still had to read the story in the basal every week and work on other skills that were taught in the story. I was glad when the last two stories were actually teaching cause and effect.

During the first week, I noticed the students thought that this was just another week and at first they didn't really get the concept after all the read alouds and examples that I gave. A few students started picking it up quicker than others. Once I laid out the 30 day plan for them and they realized that they were going to work on it for a month through different lessons and activities, they began to take interest in learning the concept. I explained to them that they would be tested on cause and effect every week, but the test wouldn't be hard. I explained that we would be climbing a learning ladder. This seemed to ease their tensions. They began to develop self-confidence and feel like they could actually learn the concept.

By the second week, I began to implement the levels of learning. Allowing students to work in pairs motivated them to engage in learning the tasks. I also gave them some hands-on activities which they always enjoy doing. At the end of the second week some students started blurting out answers because they were so proud that they actually knew the correct answers. I had to remind them to raise their hands to give an answer and to please be patient and wait to be called on by the teacher. For the first time, I saw smiles on the faces of students that had not smiled all year. Learning was becoming an enjoyable task for them. When I saw this, I was really pumped up and ready to go.

In week three, I started to wonder how they were going to perform on the state test that was in two weeks. There were so many skills that they needed to know to pass this state test. I continued to test them informally. I could tell that the informal assessments were giving me the information that I needed to know. This group of low readers was actually beginning to learn cause and effect. When I administered the summative reading test on cause and effect at the end of week three, 14 out of 18 students performed with 80 to 100 percent accuracy. This was the proof for me that 30 day plans really work.

During week four, I was just extending the skill to a higher level by asking the students to provide the cause or the effect by writing it down. The cause or effect was no longer there, they had to think it up on their own to prove to me that they understood the concept. I also changed the materials from stories to informational text because it is harder for them to determine cause and effect due to lack of background information in science and social studies. Again, I helped them learn how to find the information in content area texts. At the end of week four, all 18 students scored 80 to 100 percent on the summative assessment.

My goal was accomplished. When I gave my summative assessments weekly, I felt confident that this was an accurate test to assess their learning of the skill that I taught. When I finished the 30 day plan, the students were really motivated to learn. The next week, we started reviewing and I gave a lot of practice tests for the big test. As the test day neared, I noticed some of the students began to get nervous and to panic. I could sense fear had fallen on most of the students in the room. I had to have a pep talk with them two days in a row and reassure them that their hard work had paid off and that they were now prepared to take this test. I had to keep telling this class of last year's failures that they had worked hard. I told them to "Pat yourself on the back for your hard work; you are ready for this test."

At the time this book was published Ms. Jones was waiting to hear about the results of her students on the state tests. I believe Ms. Jones has saved her students from academic failure.

The reflections presented in this chapter so far are representative of teachers' working in high need situations. We've also found that 30 day and weekly plans as part of the *Student Engagement Framework*, gain the same type of results with veteran teachers in high performing schools. The next two reflections come from two veteran teachers.

Ms. Caddell and Ms. Strength are first grade teachers. Both recently received National Board for Professional Teaching Standards Certification and successfully completed a master's degree with a specialization in reading. They developed a 30 day plan and weekly plans and implemented them in their classrooms. Ms. Caddell focused on word problems, and Ms. Strength focused on writing. Let's start with Ms. Caddell. Her 30 day learning target was "solve word problems using accurate calculations" (see plan on page 77).

When I first sat down to create this plan I stared at a blinking cursor for quite some time. Honestly, I have never put this much thought into a math lesson. Our curriculum is very cut and dry – here's the worksheet for the focus – Done! I guess I shouldn't be quick to admit that, but I'm sure that is exactly what is happening in most elementary classrooms in our county. I can't be the only one!

I began to create my plan by breaking down the process of solving a word problem. I created a "tree" of some sort starting with the main focus of the word problems at the top and branching all the way down to the smallest detail such as understanding what is essential and nonessential information. This helped me develop a plan that encompassed all of these necessary skills.

My focus the first two weeks – I wanted to give my students the tools they needed to decipher what was important and what was not. I also wanted them to understand the key phrases found in word problems and how these would help them solve the problem. The subsequent two weeks included helping students solve the word problems. At this point in the process I thought my students needed to see the process from beginning to end every single time; if not I thought they might be confused. But, I would just have to wait and see if my thought held true as I implemented the plan.

Because I had spent so much time thinking through my instruction and specifically planning for my students to learn, I felt excited to begin teaching it!

When I began teaching, I felt an immediate slow-down! I worried I was taking too long and began worrying that I wasn't covering as much as I should. However, when I stopped and stepped back to watch my students, I realized how well they were responding to the change of pace. They were asking more questions, becoming more engaged, and appearing more confident. In the past, when working on word problems, I always had those few students who shut down. Beginning at THE beginning was wonderful for these students in particular.

In week one and two, I spent a lot of time putting up examples of word problems on the document camera, and I called up students to help me find important information. I used this format throughout the unit using bright markers to highlight questions, key phrases, and important numbers. I gave students copies of the pages I displayed and they used colored pencils to follow along and make their own markings. This form of interactive teaching helped my students better understand the task at hand and prepared them for performing on their own.

In weeks three and four, my students worked in pairs and groups daily. This is such a confidence builder and it allows students to learn from each other. It also freed me up to walk amongst the groups and assess their progress and provide immediate feedback. I noticed something spectacular – my students' growing excitement for "word problem time." Because I was teaching them in smaller chunks that they could learn to master and build upon, they were eager to do more! They proved this by performing at high levels on the assessments I gave.

I assessed my students daily through questioning and checking daily assignments. I did not assign a grade to their daily practice papers; rather I looked over them to gain insight on what I should teach the next day. This was a new approach for me in my math instruction. I did not grade their daily papers before, but I also did not use them to guide my instruction. I just wrote "minus 8" and went on with the next lesson in the book. By using formative assessment information through questioning, observation, mini-conferences I learned where my students truly were in the process and how I could take them all the way through.

I gave my students a summative assessment once a week. I created my own test that represented my learning targets for the week. Rather than expecting them to solve a word problem in the first week, they only had to identify important components of the word problem and explain them to me. We did this orally and one on one. By week two, I added circling the question and underlining the key phrase in the question. In week three, they had to draw a picture and/or write the math sentence and in week four we put it all together. They solved the word problems. This proved to be very effective for all my students. They were able to build on each step and show me what they had learned that week! Each week, at least 85% of the students were making A's and B's on these assessments!

I made a point to meet with my students at least three times a week to discuss their progress. I gave immediate feedback during question/answer time practiced as a whole class. I also spent time reviewing the test and going over each question, spending extra time with the ones that presented the most problems for them to solve. One of my precocious students asked me while we were engaged in a mini conference, "Why didn't you do this before, Mrs. Caddell? I just stared at him for a minute and responded, "I have no idea." It meant so much to my students to know where they were in the learning process and how to get to the next place.

I was amazed to see the excitement for learning and the level of performance when I took a step back, broke down the concepts, and taught to my students' needs. One group of students that benefited tremendously was ESOL students. They struggle with word problems because of the language barrier. Because I was so detailed and spent a great deal of time on each aspect they were able to fully understand before I moved on.

We have so much material to cover and I always feel pressure to COVER it! Now that I have executed this plan and have seen results with my students, I don't think I am going to feel as much guilt or pressure. Rather, I will do what gets results. All of my students have a firm understanding of word problems at the first grade level. I feel confident I have created a firm foundation that will stay strong as they encounter this skill in the upper grades.

As witnessed, Ms. Caddell reports tremendous benefits for her students – they achieved and became more engaged. Also, her students visibly saw a difference and expressed that they liked the change. Consider an additional example. Similar to Ms. Caddell, Ms. Strength's excitement grew as she watched her students become more engaged. Remember, neither teacher is a novice. They represent two experienced high performing teachers who believe that continuing to learn and grow makes them better and better teachers. Ms. Strength's 30 Day Plan learning target was "demonstrate improved paragraph writing skills."

> *I decided against using a commercial program or materials to create my own examples, prompts and rubrics. I did not much vary in the writing skills I taught in the past, but my approach and organization was very different. I began with a list of skills I typically work on and sequenced them by complexity and the order they need to be applied. It was challenging to make some assumptions about what students would need, but still be detailed enough to provide a roadmap for instruction. Planning was time-consuming and detailed at the beginning of the 30 Day Plan, but helped me appropriately scaffold activities and plan the amount of focus for different skills.*
>
> *I chose to assign writing buddies. By pairing students for an extended period of time, they were able to develop trust in each other and to learn how to manage their learning in their paired groups. I selected students who had similar interests avoiding friendships, which allowed me to tailor prompts and conferences to be meaningful and interesting to diverse groups of students.*
>
> *There were several materials and activities that I think influenced the success of this unit. I have to admit – I wasn't initially sold on the idea of displaying learning targets to first graders because of their limited reading ability. The first week, I just listed the targets and read them aloud to students, but didn't interact with them much. By the second week, I found myself writing the targets at the beginning of our writing time in class, explaining what each learning target meant, discussing why it was important and connecting how targets built on our focus the previous week. It made a tremendous impact when students knew where we were heading and they were much more invested in working on their writing. It was like giving them a step-by-step treasure map!*
>
> *Another positive strategy was using a "gradual release of responsibility" model to build success and independence. It was time consuming in the beginning and much of our focus was on discussing and understanding examples. I was concerned that students weren't producing tangible evidence of their learning during the first few days as we talked about writing buddies. As we moved through the plan, I was able to see the rewards of allowing students to collaborate before attempting a new target independently. Sharing specific*

learning goals and allowing much more time for practice and discussion were both positive steps with this plan.

But, the part of the 30 Day Plan project that I had never attempted before became the most valuable to me. This was my first attempt at a writing reflection journal for students to explain in their own words the skills that were important to them and how they individually understood them. In the past, I have used a writer's notebook as a portfolio or collection of writing material, but had not asked them to write about their new understandings of the writing process prior to this unit. Through reading their reflections, I was able to assess if student errors were due to a misunderstanding. I could, then, group students who needed re-teaching before the next class activity. Their journals and reflection pages became the written evidence I was seeking to formatively assess individual students and track their growth over time. With better insight, I was able to see where misunderstandings were occurring and formulate a plan to re-teach.

Student collaboration was a big part of the success of my 30 Day Plan. Using authentic beginning writings and allowing students to guide each other was very effective in both their skills and attitude about writing. I became a facilitator during our writing workshop time. Students learned to talk to each other and edit their peer writings rather than look to me for the "right answer." I have always felt that peer tutoring was an effective teaching strategy, but had not had a lot of success in using it with such a young age group before this unit. Instead of grading a writing to give information to parents about the specific strengths and weaknesses evidenced in the assignment, the students were taking ownership and responsibility for their learning!

I am proud of my first attempt at 30 Day Plans! I saw great gains in writing over a small window of time. All students' writings progressed despite their individual writing proficiency levels before we began the unit. Some of the writing targets were not flexible enough for my struggling writers to fully understand, apply and master independently. I needed to provide more scaffolding and small group work with more struggling writers. In previous years, I would describe my student writing skills as proficient, but dull. I taught writing plans as a formula to organize writing that often zapped their creativity and interest levels. Using a 30 Day Plan model helped me address the features that are found in similar writing, but also teach the diversity that can be found among great writers.

My students engaged in writing workshop with an eagerness and positive attitude. Students often have been eager to participate in a class discussion, but showed much less willingness to write independently. Using learning targets to scaffold learning, students seemed to feel better prepared to take risks and write. Pairing writing buddies helped students step outside their comfort zones and try new things. They had a peer to turn to for questions and celebrations along the way. I was able to help students help each other. This approach felt very student centered instead of teacher driven.

I offered two first grade examples, one in math and one in writing. The approaches and processes used in first grade can easily be transferred with a little tweaking to fit various grade levels. Ms. Atkins showed student learning results produced by high school students facing social and academic struggles. From elementary to high school, teachers who apply the *Student Engagement Framework* have witnessed more engaged students and higher classroom achievement. Consequently, these teachers are re-engaged and see value in the differences they are making in their students' lives.

BOTTOM LINE

Bottom line - teachers integrating the *Student Engagement Framework* into their classrooms achieve student learning results. Ms. Tow, a 4th grade teacher, is one of many teachers who speak about how learners become engaged and achieve at higher levels. She writes,

Looking back on the 30 days, I witnessed an increase in motivation and engagement. Every day I wrote the day's learning target on the board and the students were genuinely excited to see what was planned for the day. They were more willing to listen and follow along with the instructional activities. With the weekly measures and the end of the unit measure calculated at the end of the 30 day period of instruction, my class average was 89. Observationally, my students are talking more about their reading and are more energized about comprehension strategies.

We want students to enter our classes each day as owners rather than renters of learning. I hope this book refocuses the way we as teachers judge our effectiveness. Students struggle with learning on their own – they depend on us to create classrooms that focus first and foremost on how well students learn. When we follow the *Student Engagement Framework*, our students are engaged, confident, and successful. We make these three outcomes our intent and focus.

Teachers who effectively apply this process make great differences in the lives of students and their parents. Teachers know they taught well when students are engaged learners - meaning their students successfully achieve one learning target at a time as they climb the learning ladder to success.

I end with the reflection about the *Student Engagement Framework* from a teacher-in-training, Ms. Frite. She applied her 30 Day Plan in a 3rd grade classroom. Why do I end with her story? Think if all the teachers we prepared wrote these words about their experience "teaching" our young people. Education would be reformed.

> *I have the unique position of taking this class as a pre-service teacher, so the opportunity to be in a classroom that this project presented was enticing to me. Since I have not had the experience of following a designated curriculum or teaching within the parameters of a school or district, I felt open to the possibilities I would encounter teaching a benchmark through the plan I created. Deciding which benchmark to teach was easy because I have tutored numerous students in Special Education who struggle with learning to recognize and rely upon a story's order of events to further their reading comprehension. I chose this benchmark: The student will determine explicit ideas and information in grade-level text, including chronological order of events.*
>
> *As I began writing my 30 day plan, I was surprised by how much time I spent thinking about the steps necessary to ensure students would reach the learning target that I created. Initially I was concerned about breaking down the steps too far; I thought I might bore the students by making the first week's learning targets too simple. As I planned my first week of learning targets I thought about each of the students in this class and realized that some may hit the target very quickly and others will relish the chance to start at the very beginning of this benchmark and progress forward only when they mastered each small skill sets required to reach the full benchmark.*
>
> *I felt like my first day of instruction with the 30 Day Plan would be successful because I approached it with a positive attitude and I was armed with a lively pace. Included in my plan was time for introducing the learning target, teaching the target, student practice, and formative assessment to pinpoint where each student landed in relation to the learning target. Day one of week one went almost as I had expected. The "curve ball" was that this class had already covered chronological sequence of events earlier in the year, and the students were quick to tell me they had already learned what I was presenting. Since I have spent most of the year "pushing in" to this class weekly, I had a good rapport with the students, and they were convinced of my explanation for reviewing a valuable topic. As we moved through the learning tasks toward the learning target, some students did arrive sooner than others, but all were engaged and seemed excited to see their progress toward the target as revealed in the formative assessments. Some students stated, "This is easy" as they worked on learning tasks the first week, maybe*

because they learned the material when it was previously presented. The formative assessment that worked really well with the students was the "thumbs up" if you have it, "thumbs down" if you need help. Four students in particular, who often do not wish to draw attention to themselves, eagerly gave me "thumbs down" and were smiling as I gave them a quick reteach of their confusion. I also found it interesting how helpful neighboring students were to those who gave me the "thumbs down" sign. In the few moments it took for me to circulate among the struggling students they were already receiving additional instruction with examples and non-examples from students next to them. Seeing this action reminded me that I don't necessarily have to provide the additional help for students; they can use a buddy system to close gaps revealed in formative assessments.

In the following weeks, I did revise my plans to allow for six sentences to be chronologically sequenced instead of four because I felt like this class of students demonstrated the need for the extra practice six required. Like the students said, the first week was too easy. I also continued to use "thumbs up and down" as a formative assessment because the students who needed help, but won't ask for it responded so openly to the technique, thus receiving extra teaching as needed. I noticed that some students needed more confidence in their answers, not necessarily more instruction to reach the learning targets. The students who lacked confidence in their work eagerly approached the learning tasks that incorporated self checking or partner checks for accuracy. By using formative assessments with each daily learning target I could tell when students were ready to move to the next phase.

When students felt confident in their mastery of the weekly learning targets they were eager to take the summative assessment attached to the target. The weekly summative assessment scores steadily increased from 83% to 96%. Although I'm not able to record the grades students received on the summative assessments I did score them, included constructive written feedback, and returned them to the students. Judging from student comments and smiling faces I concluded that many students felt proud of their good scores. Of course there were also students who didn't seem concerned with their score, but even they looked interested in reading my written comments to them.

Knowing that chronological order of events was a review topic for these fourth graders makes my results even more enlightening. The initial formative assessment revealed a few students who needed more learning and practice with the topic. By breaking the standard down to small sequential steps toward the big idea, followed by formative assessments, students who previously had not learned the topic progressed toward the learning target. During the 30 Day Plan I never felt like I was leaving a student behind as I plowed ahead with a lesson, which is how I felt when I substitute taught in classrooms and was asked to cover too much content material without enough teaching and practice for some students to genuinely learn.

Teachers are the most important factor that affects student learning. We are lucky to have so many good teachers who are eager to improve their teaching skills and re-energize their will when they learn and practice strategies that help their students become engaged learners. I am lucky to do work that allows me to be with teachers and witness the difference they are making in students' lives. Teachers deserve opportunities to do worthwhile work and to receive worthwhile development – they are students' heroes.

Who's Engaged? Hopefully you will be with your students every day. Continue to help your students climb the learning ladder.

REFERENCES AND NOTES

1. Studer, Q. (2008). *Results that Last*. Hoboken, New Jersey, John Wiley & Sons.
2. Black, P. & Wiliam, D. (1998), Inside the black box: raising standards through classroom assessment , *Phi Delta Kappa, 80*(2), pp. 139 – 144.
3. Sadler, R. (1988). Formative assessment: Revisiting the territory. *Assessment in Education: Principles, Policy & Practice,* 5, 77-84.
4. Marzano, R.(2003). *What works in schools: Translating Research Into Action.* Association for Supervision and Curriculum Development.
5. Stiggins, R. (2007). Assessment through the student's eyes. *Educational Leadership, 67* (8), 22-26.
6. Nater, S. & Gallimore, R. (2006). *You Haven't Taught Until Students Have Learned; John Wooden's Teaching Principles and Practices.* Morgantown, WV: Fitness Information Technology.
7. Studer, Q. (2008). *Results that last.* Hoboken, New Jersey, John Wiley & Sons. Quint speaks about the four phases of competencies in the Studer Group two day presentations, *Take You and Your Organization to the Next Level.* A diagram of the phases was created in this book to present a clear picture of the phases that Quint refers to in his presentations.
8. Senge, P. (2006). *The Fifth Discipline: The Art and Practice of the Learning Organization.* Double Day.
9. Bloom, B. (1956). T*axonomy of educational objectives: The Classification of Educational Goals, Handbook 1: Cognitive Domain.* New York: Longmans, Green.
10. Chappuis, J. (2005). Helping students understand assessment. *Educational Leadership, 63*(3), 39-43.
11. Pilcher, J. & Largue, R. (2009). *How to Lead Teachers to Become Great.* Firestarter Publishing.
12. Rath, T. (2004). The best ways to recognize employees, *Gallup Management Journal.* In addition, Gallup's 30 year research on employee engagement provides a foundation for the way we define individual engagement that can be translated to various settings.
13. In two books written by Quint Studer (*Results that Last and Hardwiring Excellence*) he specifically describes how to apply rounding to lead people to achieve organizational outcomes. We apply his thoughts to suggest that teachers could "round" on students to gather information about learning from students.
14. Angelo, T. & Cross, P. (1993). *Classroom Assessment Techniques: A Handbook for College Teachers.* Jossey Bass Higher Education and Adult Education Series.
15. Six Trait Writing Tool created by the Northwest Regional Laboratory now known as Education Northwest (educationnorthwest.org)
16. Pilcher J., Largue, R., & Ellis, H. (2010). *Aligning Instruction to Standards: Just Ask Andie* (2nd Edition). Institute for Innovative Community Learning at <u>whosengaged.net</u>

ABOUT THE AUTHOR

Janet Pilcher has a Ph.D. in Measurement and Evaluation from Florida State University, a master's degree in educational leadership from the University of West Florida and a bachelor's degree in business from Florida State University.

Dr. Pilcher began her education career as a high school math teacher and tennis coach. Upon completion of her doctoral degree she became a faculty member at the University of West Florida. There Dr. Pilcher was the associate dean and then dean of the College of Professional Studies for 11 years. During her tenure, she was the first dean at the university to lead faculty to develop online programs that today are some of the largest programs on campus. While at UWF she landed over 17 million dollars of state and federal grants to create technology-driven learning environments for teachers and educational leaders. She has published a number of research articles in reputable journals that focus on accountability, assessment, and critical issues in today's society.

Five years ago she launched an entrepreneurial center affiliated with the university that has tripled in gross income each year and runs with about a 30% profit margin. In four years, Dr. Pilcher led her staff to achieve a goal to be a million dollar revenue generating center. TeacherReady®, the center's premier virtual program, prepares second career teachers who live all over the world. Currently the program certifies teachers in 20 states and over 10 countries. The success of this program has positioned the center to be a leading research and development hub for preparing new teachers to be successful in classrooms. The university center is in the process of becoming an independent start-up company supported by Studer Group and with a continued partnership with the University of West Florida.

This past year, Dr. Pilcher began a business partnership with the Studer Group to work with school districts in the United States to execute Evidence-Based Leadership™. Her goal is to work with the EBL model to increase student achievement, improve workplace environments for teachers and staff, and increase parent satisfaction with their children's schools. Her latest book with co-author, Dr. Robin Largue, was recently published by Firestarter Publishing, *How to Lead Teachers to Become Great*. This book helps leaders understand what is expected of them by teachers and for teachers to understand what they can expect of leaders so that schools can achieve student learning results and have engaged teachers and satisfied parents.

Dr. Pilcher lives on and manages a 16 acre family farm in Beulah, Florida, a place that has historical roots throughout generations in her family.

Contact Dr. Pilcher at janet.pilcher@studergroup.com

RESOURCES

- Purchase *Who's Engaged: Climb the Learning Ladder* to See and access other resources at <u>educatorready.com</u> or contact

    Janet Pilcher
    <u>janet.pilcher@studergroup.com</u>
    850.454.7705

- Purchase *How to Lead Teachers to Become Great* at <u>www.studergroup.com/education</u>

- Access free resources for teachers at <u>teacherready.net</u>

- Encourage someone you believe would make a great teacher to become one. Ask them to visit <u>teacherready.org</u> to learn more about being prepared to teach and receive certification.